Straggle

Also by Tanis MacDonald

Poetry
Fortune
Holding Ground
Mobile
Rue the Day

Nonfiction
The Daughter's Way: Canadian Women's Paternal Elegies
GUSH: Menstrual Manifestos for Our Times (co-editor)
Out of Line: Daring to Be an Artist Outside the Big City

Straggle

Adventures in Walking While Female

Tanis MacDonald

WOLSAK
& WYNN

Published by Wolsak and Wynn Publishers
280 James Street North
Hamilton, ON L8R2L3
www.wolsakandwynn.ca

Editor: Noelle Allen | Copy editor: Andrew Wilmot
Cover and interior design: Jen Rawlinson
Cover image: Seamless pattern with autumn forest background stock illustration © Okta Libriansyah putra
Author photograph: John Roscoe
Typeset in Minion and Ruddy
Printed by Brant Service Press Ltd., Brantford, Canada

10 9 8 7 6 5 4 3 2 1

The publisher gratefully acknowledges the support of the Ontario Arts Council, the Canada Council for the Arts and the Government of Canada.

Library and Archives Canada Cataloguing in Publication

Title: Straggle : adventures in walking while female / Tanis MacDonald.
Names: MacDonald, Tanis, author.
Description: Includes bibliographical references.
Identifiers: Canadiana 20220166366 | ISBN 9781989496534 (softcover)
Subjects: LCSH: Walking—Psychological aspects. | LCSH: Women hikers. | LCSH: MacDonald, Tanis. | LCGFT: Essays.
Classification: LCC GV199.58 .M33 2022 | DDC 796.51082—dc23

For the soft ones

Choose your instrument, asking only:
can you play it while walking?

Jay Griffiths, *Wild: An Elemental Journey*

Contents

Introduction

Dissolved by Walking

I'm on a solo walk through a part of Winnipeg where a high school friend once lived. I'm back for a few days in the city where I grew up, and now I'm doing what I often do: walking to let multiple associations rain down on me. I'm deep into my ragged and rattled memory of a place, which I like to think of as Barbara Kingsolver has described it: memory as "related to truth, but not its twin." I'm looking for my old friend's house and trying to recall details. It was one of the smallest on the block, I think, and stucco with painted yellow accents – what would have been called "harvest gold." I pass the house, or think I pass it, and am turning my memory over and over like a worn sock, wondering if I can mend it, when I see a path to the river. It leads through some bushes, the grass worn down to dirt by neighbourhood kids and dogwalkers. I push past some bushes and enter a clear space with a big sign warning of the dangers of getting too close to the riverbank, which I read and then, of course, move around to get closer to the river. The Assiniboine River is big and beautiful, flowing in its muddy way. I grew up walking along this river, and going to bush parties beside it. I miss having easy river access where I live now, in Waterloo, Ontario, and I love that I found this neighbourhood spot. I bend to take a photo and then I slip in the mud behind the sign. I slide a few feet toward the riverbank but dig in before my legs go over. I'm prone and alone, with muddy knees and hands, out of view of passersby but well in view of a sign that told me explicitly not to do exactly this. I get up, crawl carefully back to safety and work on brushing the worst of the mud away.

I spend the rest of the day a bit grimy, intentionally not returning to the place I was staying for clean clothes. I wanted to live with the consequences of my actions – a small price to pay. The dirt on my jeans reminded me that to walk, especially alone, especially if you are not cis-male, abled and white, is always a risk. The territory can be as familiar as the taste of your own spit or as strange as a moonscape, but walking invites newness, which involves delight and apprehension, though not always in equal measure. Walking invites thinking differently, breathing differently; it invites the vagus nerve to work its electric magic on your nervous system.

Not too long ago, I was out walking near my place in Waterloo and heard an amazing voice belting out a run of notes. I found the singer, a young Black woman in a snug green toque and camouflage-patterned tights, striding along the park's perimeter, just letting her voice soar. I can't sing like that kick-ass woman who I only saw for thirty striding seconds, but she reminded me to hum as I went, and that walking makes the private public, sometimes in beautiful ways. I liked her sense of risk and her sense of place; it's hard, some days, to access either – to love the local when the local doesn't love you back.

The much-quoted Latin phrase *solvitur ambulando* – "it is solved by walking" – always makes me a bit suspicious. Walking can give us a new perspective on what ails us, and some things can be solved by walking it out, walking it off or walking away, but it depends on the problem. Who is it who is doing the walking? Where and how? Does "walking well" necessarily involve speed or distance or achievement? Many books about walking lean toward adventure or distance hiking – hiking to campsites in remote areas, going on pilgrimages, endurance hikes, scientific hikes, even heritage hikes. There are fewer books about walking written by someone like me: a woman with a demanding trauma brain, more than a decade of chronic pain, an intense need for solitude and whose adventures are small. While it would be unfair to say that all books about walking written by white men are inevitably about feats of strength, books like Robert Macfarlane's *Underland* or George Monbiot's *Feral* suggest that the wild is about achievement, muscularity and encounters with the masculine self – and women who are not elite athletes are not invited.

But there's another gathering going on and that's the party I'm inviting you to: women walking. In her book *Wanderlust*, Rebecca Solnit notes that it is "the most obvious and the most obscure thing in the world, this walking that wanders so readily into religion, philosophy, landscape, urban policy, anatomy, allegory, and heartbreak." I agree, and to that list I will add the possibility of nature writing as disability writing, as a feminist world view and as an assault survivor narrative. These inclusions seem obvious to me, but survivor stories in nature are too often framed as cautionary tales and only cautionary tales, or the reverse, stories of individual triumph that don't address the larger question of spaces being both welcoming and dangerous for women, LGBTQA folks, people of colour and disabled people. But as soon as you begin to look for these accounts, you will find that they surface everywhere – from the pair of male hikers who menaced Cheryl Strayed in *Wild*, to ecology professor and self-named "Black birder" J. Drew Lanham's discussions of how racist violence limits his birdwatching, to UK critic and disabled walker Morag Rose's choice of "anarcho-flaneuse" as an identity to emphasize that the act and performance of walking, as well as walking space, should be accessible to everyone. For the past decade, especially since my own mobility has become a daily negotiation, the questions of who is walking and how have become more and more pointed.

I grew up in Winnipeg, close to the edge of the city, where there was still prairie. Most of that prairie is gone from the city limits now, but there was a time when I could bike down a paved path through the oak and poplar forest close to where I lived and if the wind was from the right direction, I could smell bison, a fluctuating herd of ten to fourteen animals penned in on the west side of the zoo. Stopping in the forest with the aspen leaves trembling, I always wondered why the bison didn't just break down the fence and light out for the prairie only half a kilometre away. In time, more bison were housed only a few kilometres away, at FortWhyte Alive, the environmental education preserve on the southern edge of the city. They must have been able to smell the bison in the zoo, and the bison in both fenced-in sites must have felt the bone memory of the spectacular herds of bison who roamed wild here until the 1880s. This swing of placement/displacement is what Jane Jacobs would call a "problem in organized complexity," or more plainly spoken, the ongoing force of colonialism on our cities, our walking and the flora and fauna that we move among.

Decades after I moved away from the Prairies, Cree poet Louise Bernice Halfe told me that the Cree word *wahkohtowin* is often trans-lated as *relationship* but its meaning is more complex, and it's better to think of it as *relationship plus energy*. Together, the combination of relationship plus energy generates a "crooked, bent-over way with all the crooks and crannies within a relationship that encompasses energy." That "bent-over way" reminds us to pay attention to and be in concert with all forms of life: land, the four elements, people and animals, plants – all in those crannies of a complex system of intricate relationships. I remember Louise saying once, "I wake up with the dawn and I walk in this crooked way and then I come back and tell you with this energy." I love that Cree concept of the bent human life in those pockets and crannies, of vibrant life all existing together. I am also encouraged that writers like Eva Mackey, in her book *Unsettled Expectations*, note that discovering and remaining in a state of uncertainty about the land is a vital tool to use when choosing a respectful way to be. I also like how Stó:lō writer Lee Maracle puts it *My Conversations with Canadians*: "No one became curious about how Canadian law became the law that dominated the landscape. No one was curious about what was here before." I am curious, and uncertain, and have come to believe that these are good positions, positions a walker ought to consider when leaving their home. Not sure if you belong on this piece of land? Unsure about what *belong* might mean in this context? Uncomfortable when hearing about the ways your favourite parks and natural areas were formed and are maintained by some very good practices as well as some harmful colonial decisions? Yeah, me too. Wherever I walk, I know it's my responsibility to consider the history of colonization in Canada and not just be overwhelmed by the beauty of the land. Haudenosaunee scholar Susan M. Hill writes in *The Clay We Are Made Of: Haudenosaunee Land Tenure on the Grand River* that the mutual obligations of Indigenous and non-Indigenous people living here creates a chain of life and respect and, in her words, "it is time to polish that chain and commit to never letting it tarnish again." Uncertainty is a good learner's position. That won't be solved by walking, but individual locomotion sharpens my curiosity about what it means to step on this piece of ground, then this one.

Straggle is a book about imperfect walking in imperfect situations: sometimes dangerous, sometimes defiant, sometimes just trying to get down the street. What if walking is as much a problem as it is a pleasure? And what if that problem could become a pleasure if we walk with it? British psychogeographer Phil Smith suggests that any walk at any time has the potential for any walker to "walk at a distance from the 'norms' that operate perniciously in our societies"

– an excellent point. Smith's psychogeographical work urges us to "get outside and become outsiders" in our embodiment, to "disrupt the optical flow" of looking at screens all day, or books, or any object only a metre or two away from our faces. I'm book- and screen-bound a lot, and feel more and more like there's an excellent reason why "myopic" is not a compliment. But it is also surprisingly easy to step outside while staying an insider, mired in your own context, refusing to look or listen. I think of the young father who passed me with his family, more than twelve feet of distance between us on a wide trail; he glared at me as I walked by and refused to return my greeting. Perhaps he thought I had no business being in his roving living room. Walking takes up space, both psychic and physical.

Walking is a vehicle for presence. There is work and joy and pain in being here, feeling the ground roll beneath my feet. I wanted to write a book about my paradoxical experiences of walking, about being strong, female, fragile, smart, a perpetual beginner and a straggler in the speed-obsessed twenty-first century. *Straggle* is a book about what happens when someone like me puts on her shoes.

The Deer in the Painting

White-tailed deer stood completely still in the painting by Clarence Tillenius, downstairs in the rec room. Arrested while stepping through copper autumn or deep snow, always two does with one stag, his head raised and staring at the artist, who painted him looking at us, his antlers the forward-curving beam that holds up the sky. Chest deep, the body's cliff. Foot-long tail less like a flag than a flying middle finger with a stiff-legged start. Some time much later, when you are grown, one of the does finds you. She slips like smoke between the trees, an appearing act. An ear turned ninety degrees, head rising on a smooth column – the arc of seeing you. Her long hundred-yard stare, like she's not even a little afraid, like if you were close enough she'd kick just to see you flinch. Though you don't move, she melts into the bush: slight of hoof, sleight of hand.

We, Megafauna

One evening in Muenster, Saskatchewan, a large white-tailed doe was browsing in a kitchen garden. As my group of walkers approached, all of us on a writing retreat, a few kept chatting away. The doe's head came up. She saw us, and for a second, I saw the flex of her powerful flanks before she whirled and ran. She lit down the gravel road too fast and light to leave even a wake of dust, then sailed over a wire fence like she had wings. I loved that she knew exactly how to get away.

*

When I write about seeing my non-human neighbours, I do it to feel my own dumbfoundedness, to let the breadth and depth of species loneliness roll through my veins instead of mashing it into a tight ball of anxiety in my gut. Potawatomi biologist and environmentalist Robin Wall Kimmerer defines *species loneliness* as the isolation human beings feel from other living beings, an isolation that we have constructed with our fear, arrogance and "our homes brightly lit against the night." Adding to that loneliness are the ways capitalist modernity has devolved to try to convince each of us of the historyless-ness and anywhere-ness of our surroundings.

I am conscious that every day it is a fight against this kind of commercialized sameness, to know where I am and note what I see in order to push through the welter of unconsciousness. Luckily, I am unsophisticated enough that I get excited seeing birds and animals. It stimulates my vagus nerve, that wanderer of the nervous system that touches the heart, the lungs and the stomach. To be unabashedly excited about the everyday is to be in good health. Too much boredom injures the heart.

Walking reminds me that I have a body. My body propels me through spaces. It gets wet feet, it gets cold, it sees or doesn't see animals and birds. It carries the brain's agenda and often scuppers that same agenda. It reminds me that time is not something that I can manipulate by working faster, or bend by answering a ton of emails, or collapse by driving. Walking until I'm tired and then needing to walk back reminds me that distance does not fold into itself. Walking with a sore ankle, a painful hip and the lit match of sciatica flaring down my thigh reminds me that I am not data in action, nor am I a set of social expectations. I am a body with abilities and limitations.

*

A white-tailed doe is lying dead in the weeds by the road, killed by an automobile. The road is two lanes wide, linking parts of a suburb in Waterloo, Ontario, a small city built on what has long been the traditional territories of the Anishinaabe and Haudenosaunee peoples. The road cuts along the edge of the conservation area with a farmer's field on the other side. The road has become busier over the last ten years as more houses have been built and more deer habitat annihilated.

It's early June when I see her. She's facing the wrong way for how she must have been hit. I try to figure out the angle and force of impact. I imagine that if the car struck her late at night or early in the morning, the driver may have left their vehicle to drag her body off the road and into the weeds. Another few feet and she'd have been hidden in the taller brush. I picture the driver's panic and the unexpected weight of a large dead animal. If it was dark, the driver may have thought she was well hidden. In the light of day, however, she is very visible, her golden head and neck still graceful, the weeds wreathing her shoulders. When I drive back a few hours later, she's still there, staring a few feet past the steady flow of traffic with the disinterested gaze of the dead. There's no shoulder for me to stop on, and even if there were, what could I do? It's a dangerous curve of road for everyone, but she's the one who has paid the price. If I had been walking the footpath and come upon her that way, I would have taken a moment to stand or hunker down beside her, to grieve the violence. I wish for that as I pilot my car around the curve and into the left turn heading home.

How little time it takes to go from writing about the natural world to writing about human violence; the body of the deer like the body of a woman found in the woods. The body becomes reduced so quickly to the question of who sees her and who does not. What you see when you make an effort to look is not always beautiful. What you find in the woods or in a field or on a hillside can soothe you, but it can scare or sober you, too.

*

Remembering is a walking skill. I walk to get a sense of soil beneath my feet, and to discover when and where the land dries up or spills over into bogs and marshes that create habitats for the non-humans who live there, but I walk also to remember the history of colonialism on Turtle Island. It's important to keep in mind that not long ago, people who looked like me displaced, starved and killed people

who lived here and who listened carefully to the land. This historical and ongoing violence humbles me. I have to deny the capitalist
assumption that this land belongs to me in any way. A walk in a
conservation area is not a solution to centuries of violence against
Indigenous peoples or against women, but it is worse – much worse
– to pretend that the land is valuable only as real estate. It shouldn't
be, at this time in history, completely comfortable to walk anywhere
– a city, a small town or a preserved and managed natural area, especially for people who come from settler backgrounds.

*

Imagine an apex observer as an organism occupying the top of the
looking chain. An apex predator is not hunted, except when she is.
An apex observer is not observed, except when she is. I am observed
as I observe: by animals who move deeper into cover at the sound of
my feet on a path, by other walkers, by uniformed park staff. The observer is the observed, unless the observer takes serious measures to
stay hidden, and some do: duck hunters behind a blind, blackbirds
nesting in heavy reeds, snapping turtles at the bottom of the pond.
Some creatures hide to hunt, some to keep from being hunted.

The deer's body is gone the next day, and while I am glad that
she's been removed from the humiliation of the roadside, I know
that with that act of collection, her death becomes a statistic. She is
now just roadkill, the shrugged-over-but-accepted price of having a
conservation area so close to ever-encroaching humanity with our
houses and cars and need for speed.

The fact that I saw her from my car underlines my own complic-
ity in this blood-for-beauty exchange. I can't stop thinking about
the size of her: long-limbed and mammalian, easy to anthropomor-
phize, an animal biologists call "charismatic megafauna." Legends
and origin stories the world over are deeply embedded ways of

cultural thinking, and in these stories, humans slip like untethered souls between deer and humans, horses and humans, bears and humans. The wrath of the Greek gods was such that one wrong look or one misstep could turn a human into an animal, setting the stage for an ironic fate. Actaeon was turned to a stag, then torn apart by his own hunting dogs. Callisto was transformed into a bear and then killed by her own son in the hunt. The word *deer* is derived from the Old English *dēor*, which was not specific to the animals we now call deer but was used to refer to any wild animal, including bears, foxes, wolves and boars. Megafauna like us, but not like us.

In Pennsylvania, where the white-tailed deer is the state animal, vehicle collisions with deer are becoming so common (a one in sixty-three chance, according to *Popular Pittsburgh*) that the rhetoric has shifted to deer striking cars rather than cars striking deer. Pennsylvania is not alone, though the reported 115,000 deer-vehicle collisions in 2013 surpass the 14,000 for all of Ontario in 2018. These "deer strikes" are a huge insurance issue, and in Pennsylvania, the nomenclature is intriguing. The white-tailed deer by the highway are transformed into a paramilitary force – deer striking out, striking back. To refer to "deer strikes" is to incorporate the language of blame: *I didn't hit the deer, the deer hit me.* The automobile and driver are not culpable; they are victims in incidents where nature, red in tooth and claw (and apparently hoof), has attacked the everyday suburban demand for convenience. What happens to an apex observer who does not (or cannot) look? And why can't I find statistics of deer-vehicle collisions for where I live?

Mary Ruefle's essay "Lectures I Will Never Give" in *Madness, Rack, and Honey* considers the case of a deer "that jumped out of nowhere" toward a car in which Ruefle was a passenger. The driver, who was another writer, braked and swerved. Neither humans nor deer died in the encounter, but the incident sparked a debate between the two writers: the driver cursed at the sight of the deer and Ruefle wanted to get even closer to it. The driver suggested that the differences in their reactions could form a lesson about writing "good poems" or "bad poems." He suggested that Ruefle should tell the story to her students: "Call it the Deer Lesson and then walk out of the classroom." The act of the instructor walking out is part of the lesson, implying that there is a correct way to write a poem and students should know which to choose. But I'm not sure I would know which to choose. Ruefle, always modest, notes that she could write about the deer no other way. This is a lecture she will never give; Ruefle doesn't believe in "bad poems" the way the other poet does, nor (I'm guessing) does she believe in being told how to teach. The "Deer Lesson" is not a classroom lesson, though it may be a lesson about driving: drivers where I live are instructed with the rhyme "don't veer for deer." What would Ruefle have thought if she was at the wheel?

*

The deer by the roadside haunts me not because she was beautiful and not because of the violence of her death; she haunts me because she reminds me of the dangers of boundary crossing. Like one in five women in North America, I'm an assault survivor, and yet I go into the woods. When I say *the woods*, I almost always mean parks and managed forests, spaces that are tended to and are not especially wild; spaces that are both offered and denied to women and non-white men. The place I am talking about has groomed trails and signage pointing to picnic areas. Walking there is nothing like hacking through dense bush or survivalist camping. But despite its relative tameness, the foliage is thick and obscuring, the better to convince me I am far from home. Though barely wild, there are places in that managed forest far enough away from roads that trying to get home with a broken ankle would be a problem; places where I would not want to be alone at night.

Every walk I take is a defiance of my parents' warning to be careful because anything could happen. This is depressingly ironic, as something bad *did* happen when I was a kid; however, that crime was not perpetrated by a dark stranger in the woods but by someone my parents knew in our very ordinary suburb in a very ordinary North American city. So maybe I'm not as afraid of the woods as I ought to be. Survivor relativism tells me that the conservation area could be a place of danger, but so could my living room. You might expect assault survivors to be afraid of many things, and we often are. But it is also sometimes true that we are not afraid of things that scare other people, in part because we've lived through the unimaginable.

I go to the woods to remind myself that I live a life shaped by many ideas that are dangerous to me, and that the dangers of walking alone in the woods have the advantage of being more evident, less sneaky. The woods are not going to sweet-talk or gaslight me. The woods – cold, wet, full of unexpected encounters with forms of life I don't really understand – never pretend to be anything more than they are.

*

There's a small herd of urban deer living in the green corridor that starts near my house and scoops southeast. It took me a few years to see any deer at all. These deer are not laissez-faire about public view like the mule deer in Banff, many of whom don't even look up as you pass within a few feet. These aren't even the white-tailed deer that Daniel Coleman writes about in *Yardwork* – he spots those deer more often than not whenever he ventures out into the wild space that abuts his home in Hamilton. My local deer are shy, easily startled. My first sighting was of a large brown flank disappearing into the brush, and I thought it was a trick of the light. But I found hoofprints there, which meant that I had been walking in a thirty-acre conservation area for three years without seeing evidence of deer until then. I was either seriously inattentive or the deer were stealthy. Probably both.

But once I knew to look, I saw more; deer would coalesce, appearing from within a mix of branches and leaves and sunlight before just as quickly melting out of view as though their molecules had seeped into the undergrowth. This near-magical ability is a skill practised by white-tailed deer, I learned from Elizabeth Marshall Thomas's book *The Hidden Life of Deer*. Thomas writes that deer know precisely where their vanishing point is, the exact spot they need to get to in order to "disappear" from human sight. "Fleeing deer re-enter the woods in all sorts of places, slowing down or stopping right after they know they have disappeared," notes Thomas, adding that "to appreciate what the deer were doing we would need to enter the woods from a field and try to figure out at which point we could no longer be seen." Reading this, I was a little relieved that it wasn't just a deficiency of my eyesight. The molecule-bending ability of deer has also manifested on my walks as misrecognition, like the time I mistook a small deer nosing through the leaves for a large golden dog. The second I realized my error was a telescoping moment, like when the optometrist flicks stronger lenses into those steampunk diagnostic frames and it changes what you see. Dog; flick; deer.

My oddest deer encounter inevitably involved other humans. One evening, my partner and I were hiking up a sloped forest trail when we met a man talking to two women. He was in his early forties; a short, compact, rugged type in boots and a dark-green down vest. My partner and I discovered later that the women didn't know him, but when he and I went to pass the group on the trail, they drew us into their conversation. The man pointed down the treed slope of ash and poplar into a small valley where three or four deer were browsing, just visible and at a safe distance from us. We peered through the trees until we could make out their shapes, seeming to waver in and out of sight, and the man resumed the story he was telling the two women, which went something like this:

> Each fall, a single stag comes all the way from the deep woods in the western part of the county, a great antlered beast who walks unseen down the narrow lines of windbreak trees in farmers' fields, crossing roads in the dark of night. The stag makes his way into these woods, drawn by the overpowering scent of female deer in estrus. He impregnates the does and returns the way he came, following the lines of trees through neighbourhoods, over fields, around ponds to the deep Carolinian forest whence he came. Until next year.

I was willing to entertain the possibility of this deer procreation myth. I had never seen a stag in those woods, but since it took me three years to see the does, that proved nothing. I didn't really care if the story was true, though; I cared about why he was telling it. He was eager to pull four strangers into his Lusty Stag tale, insistent about how sperm would triumph, about how nothing – fields of crops, paved roads, new suburbs – was going to stand in its way. What I liked about the story was the long link of spaces through which the stag travelled, that the county's alignment of green spaces could mask the annual journey of a large wild mammal. If there were resident stags in the woods, the yearly appearance of an "outsider" stag could be genetically advantageous. But the story was also this guy's fantasy of procreation, made creepily boastful when he started buttonholing women in the woods so that we would know that the mighty sperm of the Lusty Stag would not be denied.

With all this doubt, something else ticks away like a metronome in the back of my head. Maggie O'Farrell's essay "Neck" has stayed with me, enough to freeze my blood on this hot summer night. It's her first-person account of an encounter with a man in a remote spot who takes advantage of her interest in wildlife to loop his binoculars around her neck from behind. This sets off O'Farrell's alarm bells and she talks her way out of his grasp and sight, only to be visited later by the police when another young woman's dead body is found just off the same path. We came upon the man telling two women the story, and when the story was done, the group broke up to go our separate ways. The two women walked ahead of us, and without discussing it, John and I dropped back to create a barrier between the women and the Lusty Stag's PR man. He might have been harmless, but he also might have had darker purposes – we could not be certain either way. We were in the woods and night was falling.

*

Quite apart from the stag-legend-as-dick-pic quality of the telling, something else bothered me about the man's story. Mysterious supernatural stags are everywhere in Celtic mythology. Cernunnos, the Horned One – often depicted as a white stag – is the Celtic god of fertility who is born at the spring equinox, marries the goddess at Beltane and dies at the summer solstice. Annoyingly, this fits the story as told by the man in the vest almost exactly: the great journey, the "marrying" of the goddess in the form of a doe, the sacrifice that makes the land fertile. The stag doesn't stay with the doe but drifts back west, the direction of the divine in many mythologies. This form of the virile stag makes hundreds of literary appearances. A magical white stag shows up in C.S. Lewis's *The Lion, the Witch and the Wardrobe*, and in Thomas Malory's *Le Morte d'Arthur* as the deer that leads Arthur and the knights to Pellinore's well. These kinds of literary references gave the man's local telling a pungent flavour of Celtic legend. But it was just too neat a fit. I was immediately suspicious, and went looking for deer stories that didn't cast female deer as victims or vessels.

I didn't have to look far; there are deer stories that are very old right here, on the Haldimand Tract, a few miles from the Grand River. The anthology *Deer Woman*, edited by Anishinaabe writer Elizabeth LaPensée and Weshoyot Alvitre, is an excellent source of retellings of this story by Indigenous women, as is Sioux-Lebanese author Paula Gunn Allen's short story "Deer Woman." The television series *Reservation Dogs* features a retelling of the Deer Woman story in the episode "Come and Get Your Love." According to Cherokee/Creek writer Carolyn Dunn, Deer Woman's pursuit of righteous vengeance pushes back against "the misuse of sexual power." Indigenous people have been telling settlers for centuries to listen to animals more, to respect them more and to acknowledge them more. The story of Deer Woman is widespread and told by many First Nations peoples all over Turtle Island, and it is not mine to retell. But Deer Woman is a formidable figure: charismatic megafauna as a woman who takes no shit.

In the far north, people have another take on powerful female deer. Danielle Prohom Olson's article "Doe, A Deer, A Female Reindeer: The Spirit of Mother Christmas" notes that in Sami and Siberian cultures, the female reindeer is a goddess figure that was once widely revered by many northern cultures but whose figure has been repressed by the patriarchal frame of Christianity. For instance, the male reindeer sheds his antlers in winter, but the doe retains hers. She's bigger and stronger, and she leads the herd in the winter. In some depictions of the Reindeer Mother, the tree of life grows from her horns and birds nest in her antlers. In other illustrations she's shown holding a glowing orb suspended between her antlers; the Reindeer Mother takes flight during the winter solstice to bring back the light of the sun.

Belief in the deer goddess was potent enough to travel widely, migrating south to become adopted into Latvian, Lithuanian, Hungarian, Russian and Scandinavian cultures, then spreading to the British Isles where the Highlands of Scotland sheltered pre-Celtic deer goddess worshippers. The concept of the doe as defenceless is undone, or at least shaken up in what Esther Jacobson calls an "ecology of belief" in doe energy. Jacobson is firm in her assertion that "the South Siberian deer was the center of a fluid symbolic system" passed from culture to culture via nomadic peoples who carried word of the deer goddess wherever they went. So potent is this doe energy and its spread across continents that Jacobsen calls it "a drama of epic proportions . . . intensely complicated by the intertwining of cultures."

Elizabeth Marshall Thomas notes that the white-tailed deer she studied on the traditional territory of the Abenaki people in New Hampshire survived because of their powerful matriarchal group structure. In studying six deer families over four years, Thomas observed that large does rule the local deer populations to the extent that a single dominant doe will determine who eats, when they eat and who gets the safest spot to sleep. As expected, a dominant doe will teach the younger deer the art of vanishing. But she also doesn't stand for any opposition among the deer families; a large dominant doe will train their older doe-daughters who remain in the group to act as enforcers to fend off interlopers, up to and including warning off stags who make any move to eat before the lead doe and her fawns.

The Deer Lesson is pointed toward bodies who appear precipitously where they are not expected; manipulating visibility is part of deer consciousness. These doe matriarchies, when they allow me to glimpse them, are excellent reminders of the creatureliness of my human body. They remind me, powerfully, that my assailant didn't kill me, and that he doesn't keep me locked inside. When I find a tuft of deer fur wedged between the barbs of a wire fence, I rub it between my fingers; it's somehow both coarse and soft. I keep it in my jacket pocket for several days, touching it as if that will help me think of a word for it.

When I walk in the natural world, I am splicing the need for rest with the possibility of risk, part of my own "ecology of belief." In the woods, I feel both my most animal self and my most human self: a blend of fiercely protective and widely creative. *Fuck you, patriarchy*, I think as I hike through the long grass or between trees. From the grasses to the insects to the birds, trees and animals large and small – the biome in all its complexity – we are here for each other, seen or unseen. This is the female forest. Walk as you would be seen.

How to Get Lost in the Woods

It's easy if you try. Take the path you know best, the well-trodden one, the one you've walked on summer and winter for ten years or more, the one Frost warns is a rut and not a path. What does he know? Shove past the deadfall barrier that was dragged there to keep out people like you and laugh while you do it. Pass the rotted lawn chair flung into the underbrush to your right, a splash of orange. The sticky hands of burrs grab green and gritty onto your jeans and hoodie, pulling you off course, trying to pull you down. You are the stubbornest creature as you shoulder through the web until you can touch the dead tree that looks like a giant tuning fork. You are the fleshiest creature, an inconvenience to yourself, trying to climb out of your body like a pit you fell into forty years ago. You hear night fall with a thud. When you turn to go back, nothing's familiar. No birdsong. The path like a basted ribbon, pulled up and gone.

How to Get Lost in Your Backyard

When the emerald ash borer moves lock, stock and wriggling barrel into your largest tree, the whole yard tips off-balance. Gutted from the inside, ashes don't go to ashes but to pulp. The day the crew comes to cut her down and grind down her stump, you are away, pushing paper.

Without the wooden lodestar, the sky flips beneath your feet when you stand, the whole yard yaws like a ship in a hurricane. You bring it back to calm seas by planting your feet where her trunk stood and reaching up. The yard rocks, then settles. From here in Ontario, with your arms raised, you can see the big poplar on the corner, hear it soughing a prairie evening. The cedars of Lebanon lean hard to the left and the black-eyed Susans turn their golden heads. You could stand here forever, dryad in jeans and flannel shirt, riding the world tide, but when a porcupine ambles out of the crawl space behind the shed, you drop your arms. The porcupine winks out like a comet. You're here again.

Animal Presence

I don't remember the name of the anthology in which I first found Denise Levertov's poem "Come into Animal Presence," but I know that I read it early in my thinking about poetry, when I was trying to read as much as I could to understand it better. I was nearly alone in this. With the possible exception of my grade eight English teacher, no one in the world at the time and place where I grew up spoke poetry. But poetry snuck up on me through my ability to memorize Bible verses for church, for school assemblies and for what used to be called "party pieces" – recitations of Robert Louis Stevenson and Robert W. Service and Robert Burns poems – for school assignments and for my parents' friends. For years I thought all poets were named Robert. I only encountered poetry when a teacher or my minister wanted me to learn a passage to perform.

But I became restive. I knew that these poems were from another era, and even as I fell in love with the strings of words ("strange things done in the midnight sun" and "Wee, sleekit cowrin' tim'rous beastie"), I was a little suspicious of how delighted adults were by my performances. I started looking for poems I wanted to read, not to memorize and recite but to learn more about words; to have for my private enjoyment rather than public performance. I mowed through all the poetry books at my local branch library; the section was small enough that this was not much of a feat. But the librarians saw what I was reading and bequeathed to me (and warned me not to tell ANYONE that they did this) some poetry anthologies that they were removing from circulation. I read them obsessively, and I suspect that I found Levertov's "Come into Animal Presence" in one of these anthologies, which were long ago jettisoned from my own roiling collection of books prior to a cross-country move. The whole poem is worth reading and obsessing over, but it's the final few lines that ring in my head. Levertov's attention to the sacredness of animal presence and the human tendency to "turn from it," an invocation she makes as seriously as an oath. Come into animal presence and do no harm. Come into animal presence and know that it's an honour. And if you are a writer, according to Sharon Olds, "this creature of [your] poem may assemble itself into a being with its own centrifugal force."

In the film *Stand by Me*, the character of twelve-year-old Gordie (played by Wil Wheaton) wakes before his friends in the woods on the final morning of a long hike. He is sitting on the railway tracks, idly sifting through pebbles at his feet when a deer steps out of the underbrush just a few feet from him. He looks; the deer looks, then steps delicately over the rails and disappears into the woods. The older Gordie narrates in voice-over: "I never told anybody about that moment. Until right now."

It's my favourite moment in the movie. It combines the willingness to tell with waiting for someone who wants to hear; with keeping a flame of private joy. Waiting for a creature of words to form a creature of flesh.

*

Creature: an animal, as distinct from a human being. Unless creature means monster, something created by a human being that is often hideous; unless creature means alien, as in from outer space, or unless it means a woman in a Victorian novel, charming creature that she is; unless it means a non-human being who causes harm; unless it is animate or inanimate, a being of anomalous aspect and uncertain mien; unless it means any living thing that can move independently; unless it means an organization under the complete control of another being. Tiny forest, small flying, of the field, multi-cellular.

*

There's an interpretative sign in the Huron Natural Area (HNA) in south Kitchener that is set by a wide groomed path through tall pines and birch, in a fairly dense planned and managed forest. The sign shows a representation of exactly what you'll see when you look up from it: the path swerving off to the left, the hollows and the trees, the spurt of underbrush, the canopy of leaves above. The sign's caption asks, "What can you see?," encouraging you to look harder, to spot the partly camouflaged birds and animals "hiding" in the drawing. The sign is meant to educate children about local fauna; it bears a strong resemblance to the kinds of seek-and-find puzzles given to children to encourage observation. There are adult versions of these sorts of puzzles: word searches, optical illusions and those once-ubiquitous "magic eye" puzzles.

The sign by the path has an answer key – a smaller black-and-white version of the forest drawing that shows the "hidden" birds and animals outlined with dotted lines and labelled: red fox, white-tailed deer, song sparrow, common crow. When we encourage children to walk quietly and practise good observation of birds and animals in the green spaces to which we bring them, we're suggesting that their careful attention will "pay off" in the sight of natural wonders. The sign, however, provides an answer for parents besieged by ultra-urban kids who complain that there's "nothing to do" when they walk in the woods. Fair enough.

In this landscape, the sign appears to suggest that not only are such creatures viewable in the woods but also that they will appear exactly where the key indicates. I catch myself doing it every time: I look at the sign's depiction of the clump of ferns from which a fox is emerging, and flick my eyes to the corresponding clump of ferns twenty metres away in hope of spotting the promised fox. Will I see the fox if I just wait, if I am patient, if I do something special with my eyes? That implicit encouragement plays on our expectations of consumer-driven display.

If you spend any time walking on land that is designated as a park or conservation area, it's notoriously easy to slip into the language of ownership. "Maybe we'll see our turkeys today," my partner says to me as we walk to the conservation area. I can hardly blame him. We've told people that at least three distinct family groups of wild turkeys live there, and we are often not believed. Nothing makes something feel more like yours than hearing it dismissed by others.

The sign in the HNA reminds walkers who's here, and suggests, usefully, that looking takes practise, the kind of practise we don't get when staring at paper or screens. The ridiculousness of the sign in the woods is mitigated in part by its necessity in a world in which words about the natural world are being excised from the dictionary. The signs that welcome walkers to the park – ironically not called a park but a "Natural Area," named for the Indigenous people who were displaced by the industry that surrounds it – were once vandalized, culture-jammed. Letters from the city name "KITCHEN-ER" were removed until the signs read "CHE," substituting Ernesto Guevara for Lord Kitchener in a way that's pretty hard to argue with. Other signs warn children that Canada geese will not submit to being touched and can be aggressive during nesting season, and that the frogs in the pond are not for catching or picking off with stones. Maybe the dotted lines in the answer key are the best way to suggest that the woods are not a zoo; the animal and birds are not on display. They live there in part because we've destroyed their other habitats and this is now their best option. They go about their business of hunting, eating, sleeping, procreating and dying, and if we see them in transit as they do any or all of that, we are lucky. The animals can choose to remain hidden, hypothesized by that dotted line, the forest's equivalent of Schrödinger's cat: both there and not there, alive in our imaginations even as they are erased from our lexicons.

*

Discussions about the power and force of looking are not new, yet they are conversations that, to my mind, seem largely unfinished, especially when we consider creaturely agency and the animal's choice (or sometimes the lack thereof) to be viewed by human eyes. Though conceptions of nakedness and nudity are very human cultural ideas, what if we applied them to how we view animals in the wild?

> To be naked is to be oneself. To be nude is to be seen naked by others and yet not recognized for oneself. . . . To be naked is to be without disguise. To be nude is to have the surface of one's skin, the hairs of one's own body, turned into a disguise which, in that situation, can never be discarded.

This famous passage from John Berger's *Ways of Seeing* illuminates the function and weight of the male gaze on women's unclothed bodies in classical painting. Berger is very clear about how these paintings position the painter/viewer as a male subject and the nude women as a knowable, collectable, displayed objects. It has been used over and over by feminist writers to reclaim the female body as a subject, and to discuss the abuse of vulnerability as a patriarchal pleasure. But what about the implications of a "nude" animal, via Berger's definition? One whose skin is turned into a disguise, one that is not seen as a subject but as an object – of desire or of derision – placed on display? When we come into animal presence, how do we recognize the animals as themselves? Practise. Lots of practise.

*

My partner and I had been recommended a trail that led to a waterfall on the Gaspé Peninsula, which is why we were, on a hot and humid July morning, climbing a muddy, sharply rising path. We slipped a lot and were knee-deep in the mud by the time we saw moose hoofprints. We had travelled all the way through New Brunswick, past many kilometres of moose fencing, and not seen one. And now, mosquito-plagued and hot, on a slippery path, mostly lost except we knew where we had left the car, I didn't need to see a moose thundering down (or up!) this slope toward us.

If anyone was on display in this scenario, it was us, animals watching from the woods on either side of the muddy path.

*

This wouldn't be complete without a zoo story. All zoo stories are about colonization, and some zoos even display animals who would be numerous on the very land that the zoo occupies if colonialism hadn't destroyed most of those animals and their environment. So it is in Winnipeg, at the bison enclosure. I stop by every time I'm in town, to get uncomfortable. I arrived once at a bison's birth by stroke of luck, stopping by their enclosure to see all the bison but one lined up against the fence just a few feet away. They watched me, warily, as I looked at the other single bison browsing in the field.

I kept clear of the fence and made no sudden movements, recalling the torn-up fence in Riding Mountain National Park as evidence of how bison could rip up structures if they felt encouraged or threatened. In Riding Mountain, I felt a lot less protected by the cattle grid I drove over on the way to the campsite. That bison herd could rip the final wires out of the fence and run onto the pedestrian path – the very one I was standing on with my boyfriend, who was the kind of guy I knew would try to outrun me in the event of a bison breakout. They didn't break out, and we didn't have to run. That was decades ago.

But back at the Winnipeg zoo, it started to rain. Why were the bison standing so close to the fence? I watched the single bison cow sequestered in the next field, saw her shiver and brace her legs, saw her lift her tail as the calf slid from her. It was pouring by the time the calf staggered to their feet and started to nurse. I was soaked to the skin. The other bison wandered away from the fence, their guardianship now abated.

*

Mature male snowy owls are pure white, so it must have been an old male who dropped out of the sky one morning as I rounded the corner of Corydon and Waverley in Winnipeg. Its flight was the soundless swoop of a master predator, an optical illusion emerging from the light wind-driven snow. Snowy owls often hunt where there is no snow, alighting on fenceposts in bare winter fields, using their acute vision to spot mice and voles moving brown amongst brown. But the sky was the grey-white of December, and when he swooped into sight, the owl was weather made flesh. He perched on the hydro pole for a few seconds. I was thirteen or maybe fourteen at the time. Was Laura with me? She lived one street over, and we often met on the walk to school, but I don't know now if we saw the owl together or if that sound, that soft exclamation, was my own awe splashing gently against the inside of my head. But I remember describing the sighting later, first at school, to my friends, and then later to my parents.

The next day, the *Winnipeg Tribune* published a photo of the owl in a cage beside another girl. He had been found in her backyard, his legs tangled in chicken wire, and her father had called Ducks Unlimited, who called the paper. The owl looked as furious as I felt – he because of his temporary captivity, and me because *he was mine.* The article quoted the other girl saying something that no kid would say: "I thought wow! A snowy owl in my own backyard! I never thought I'd see that." *Oh, come on,* I thought, full of teen-girl bitterness. *You did not think that, all sucky, gee gosh golly.* She didn't find the owl until after 3:00 p.m., but I had seen him at 8:15 a.m. I had literally seen him first.

I couldn't let it go. I showed my father the article, and he smiled and said, "So you DID see something." Far from agreeing with me that I was first past the owl-spotting post, his statement showed that he hadn't believed me to begin with. I was stung. "I saw this owl. THIS one." I jabbed the paper, startling him. I did it again, and saw with some satisfaction that my stabbing finger had creased the paper right by the girl's eye. My father drew the paper away from me. Denied the owl, denied the moment of that sight, I couldn't stand it – I was being refused that beauty because I did not have a witness. Cooler heads would've said I wasn't being denied anything; I saw what I saw whether or not anyone believed it.

But there's a reason why "pics or it didn't happen" is a saying and in that era, long before social media, people could and did shrug off reports of the amazing. They were treated as fantasy or as garden-variety lies. I was young, and the injustice of this roared through me. I waited until my father had finished with that section of the paper and then pulled it off the coffee table, feigning fascination with the headlines. I slipped into the kitchen where my mother was cooking dinner and sat at the kitchen counter, gazing at the grainy photo.

Each time I looked, the photo dissolved into pixels, newsprint ink blurring and lifting off the paper.

I was not some birding prodigy at thirteen, but Kenojuak Ashevak's painting *The Enchanted Owl* had been reproduced on a postage stamp a handful of years before, and for me, the snowy owl was both real bird and imaginative art. Despite my frequent reading of Farley Mowat's *Owls in the Family*, I knew I couldn't own or keep the owl, that he was no more mine than water was mine. But I also didn't know Levertov's maxim, that the "holiness does not dissolve," which in itself is a translation of many cultural knowledges, that animals are beings unto themselves, and that they do not exist for human amusement or our mindless consumption. The owl in the newspaper was nude, made over as an object. The owl in Ashevak's painting was a subject – itself. The owl in my head was a subject that I wanted to make into an object, and I was beaten to the punch by the girl in the paper. I was sad and jealous; my sight faltered and turned from the owl as I remembered him.

*

There is a raptor rescue centre near Mountsberg, Ontario, where a paved path from the main building leads to two-storey cages in a clearing. Joan, the rough-legged hawk, screams; Joan does not want to be looked at, and she'd take out my eyes if she could reach them. Jane, the red-tailed hawk in the next cage, flaps the half-wing she has left from colliding with a car. Jane can hear Joan. The whole park can hear Joan – her voice is a siren + a gargle + A-sharp vibrato + a woman who has had enough of some guy's bullshit. Joan shrieks and pauses, shrieks and waits. Is she Joan of Arc or is she Joan Crawford in *What Ever Happened to Baby Jane?* The screams could be mistaken for human, except they are more naked. I hardly know where to look, or if I should be looking at the hawks at all. They are there to heal, or because they can no longer feed themselves in the wild. I know this is true, and I know that hawks' screeches are as associated with territory and hunting as with alarm, so maybe Joan and Jane want me outta their patch, or perhaps they just want a piece of my flesh. Somehow, I prefer the latter.

*

It is July, and I am standing about nine metres from a white-tailed fawn on the University of Waterloo campus. He is tall and gangly enough to be an adolescent but still has a spotted coat. He browses the creekside bushes with one eye on me, neither casual nor especially cautious. After a minute, he trots over to a clump of trees where his sibling is eating, and she looks back over her shoulder at me while he eats, and then vice versa. I can hear a game of one-on-one going on behind me, across Laurel Creek, in the basketball half-court behind Conrad Grebel University College: the ball bounces and hits the backboard, and the players exclaim. Then my phone rings and both fawns look up and, incredibly, crane their necks toward the ring tone; it seems I am less scary with music. The music is an absurd invasion in the scene, and I don't want to lure the fawns closer with this artificial aid. In fact, I'm a bit freaked out that they like it and instantly picture ways an unscrupulous person could lure them to harm with it. The spell of tolerance has been broken. I thank the fawns for letting me see them and start back to my car. The fawns take a final glance over their shoulders and scamper away, making soaring arcs over the grass. Their mother appears suddenly from a hollow, and the fawns rush to her and thrust their heads beneath her belly. The doe raises her head and makes a gesture with her forelegs, similar to a human elbowing, pushing the fawns behind her. She stands tall and stares steadily at me. I thank her, too, for her generosity and her maternal ferocity. She just gives me the eye.

*

Ariel Gordon invites me for a walk in the Assiniboine Forest. I no longer live in Winnipeg, but as my parents age, I visit more frequently. I see their frailty and there's little I can do, but I fly in, sit in their house and listen. Taking a forest walk with Ariel, a long-time friend from the Winnipeg writing community, is my hour's reprieve from my father's growing grouchiness and inflexibility, from my mother's need to hang on tight to me. Growing old is not for the faint of heart. When my father is diagnosed with cancer, I arrive to take care of my mother and negotiate his care, and Ariel and I walk in the forest. When my father dies after months of treatment, I take care of all the arrangements and my mother, and I meet Ariel and we walk in the forest. When I finish my doctoral studies, I move back to Winnipeg to live with my mother for a year, teaching at my alma mater and going home each day to her loneliness. Her grief fills the house, and she and I struggle to manage it together. I thought I'd be better at this, but it turns out I am ground down by it. Trying to work through the grief together is only slightly better than either of us managing it alone. I walk in the forest with Ariel every few weeks. These walks are not a magical cure for what ails me, but they don't make it worse, and some days that's a victory.

From Ariel, I know that the Assiniboine Forest is a planned forest, but situated as it is on what was once the edge of the city and caressed lovingly with the language of conservation, the Assiniboine Forest has been rhetorically positioned as "natural," as in "naturally occurring." I always know I'm in Manitoba by the drawing of the mosquito on a post as you leave the meadow and enter the burr oak and poplar forest; the old joke that the mosquito is the official bird of the province lingers. Ariel and I talk as we walk, maybe too much. I am a poor excuse for a birder during these walks, but Ariel shows me mushrooms and moss and nest cups, and I start to experience the Assiniboine Forest as a faraway nearby, a homeplace that isn't one; as a landscape where I recognize the light and shadow as those I grew up with and am still figuring out.

After my mother dies, I stop going to Winnipeg. I don't walk in the Assiniboine Forest for three years. But I return at last for a book launch, and though I won't visit the old neighbourhood, I go to the forest with Ariel on a hot day before Labour Day, this time with University of Manitoba historian Adele Perry. They are crouched by a stand of burr oaks, just off the wooded path, looking at some fungi and I am up ahead when a coyote crosses my path in full lope like a furry train headed west – two blinks and you'd miss her. When I turn back to the others, I know they didn't see the coyote. I run to the spot where the coyote disappeared and find a narrow but definite path through the bush – a deer trail as we usually call them, but more properly, it's a trail for anyone who can fit. The coyote's long gone, vanished into the bush, but this tiny piece of evidence, this slight but distinct opening in the dense foliage, makes it possible to believe that I saw who I saw, my fleeting glance of the coyote in action.

My coyote sightings are usually at a distance, in quasi-urban industrial wastelands or half-erected housing developments, and they trot unhurriedly about, comfortable, like they couldn't care less. Sometimes they stand at a safe distance and watch me. It's been a long time since I've seen a coyote so close. I've never before seen one moving that fast. I open my mouth to call to the others, but quickly close it. I walk back to them to see their mushroom find.

*

An aerial map would show a _____ trail looping around the tall pines to the southwest and straight through a hole dug under my chain-link fence, a hot spot glowing on the map with long-eared fire. They came singly or in threes, some big and some so small they would have fit on my palm like furry stones, like little fists of meat. They were fleet as they wanted to be, so I held no _____s on my palm. Quick like a _____. Afternoons, I'd look up from my book to see a _____ two metres away. One I called Rusty because of the red fur streaking her front legs. Lucky _____ foot. Like a scared _____. Down the _____hole. What courage it takes to run and hide.

*

The day a red-tailed hawk tore a sparrow apart on the fence by the dining room window, I was in the backyard weeding and missed it all. My partner took still photos and a short video of the meal in all its tendon-ripping, skin-from-meat, blood-and-guts glory. I've seen the photos and video multiple times.

*

In "Canada's most liveable city," a mother rat and her four pups tiptoe in a straight line beneath a hedge one Sunday morning on my way to the grocery store. Grey ballerinas with long naked tails.

*

At a medieval faire, we watch two women in leather jerkins cinched with wide brown belts and sporting knee-high boots hold up birds of prey. Tethered to their wrists, a peregrine falcon with a dark head and slate wings, and a barn owl with a face like a Venn diagram. The hawk handler says, "They don't like being with us, so we can't pet them, and they won't fly to glove for food because the hawk will ball its claws up and punch its prey to break its neck before eating it, and no one wants to get behind that but we keep these big birds fed and protected so they are getting all their needs met and aren't looking for another relationship." All the couples and maybe some singles in the crowd laugh, and the hawk handler blushes. I look at my partner with his camera to his eye, twisting the lens for a close-up of the owl's white face floating in the dim tent, and know our cat will spring at our ankles when we walk in the door. She will bare her teeth and pounce, preparing for the day she succeeds in taking us down with matching thuds and eats us, beginning with our eyes. And we know, we are getting all our needs met.

*

I told Ariel about the coyote a little while ago. She believes me.

Bee City

If pollen is male, the stigma is female. Make a mullet garden: business up front, bee party in the back. The electrostatic charge of a bee makes it highly social, but if it's twelve degrees out, even your most social bee will stay home to watch Netflix and chill. If you see a bumblebee shivering as the sun goes down, you know it's not a sweat bee. You must vibrate the tomato flower and wait until the buzz hits middle C, then the deed is done. There are solitary bees you've never heard of. Like in *The Crown*, the queen controls the sex. Squash bees get up early to get a jump on the day. Only the females sting. Bats pollinate, too, just not here.

Walk This Way

Footnotes on Limps and Struts

Have you heard this one? It's an old joke, as old as vaudeville or music hall, and according to some sources, it may even be old enough to have appeared as a lazzi (a comedic set piece, a familiar "bit") in sixteenth-century commedia dell'arte. I'll bet you've seen it in one form or another: the set-up line is "walk this way," which is said by someone whose way of walking is distinct, so that the pun on "way" as both "manner" and "direction" can be maximized for the laugh. In other words, "walk this way" can mean "follow me" or "do as I am doing." And the joke is that it means both. The punchline needs a receptor for the command who arrives in circumstances where being literal minded might be an advantage – that is, they are susceptible to advice in a new place, and they take direction from someone who appears to know the milieu.

I know that I'm explaining a joke before I tell it, and I am aware that explaining a joke can drain it of its humour, but (a) I doubt that this five-hundred-year-old joke will be damaged by my tampering, and if it is, (b) I don't care, for reasons that will become clear. As a visual joke, "walk this way" is medium effective: a cheap laugh that can be striking enough if the comedian doing the imitating – walking that way – is any kind of decent mimic. Like any old joke, the laugh it garners is at least partially a bark of recognition. So it's important to acknowledge that the joke is inevitably about a disabled body and not about the morally dubious right to mimic that body for laughs. The joke is carnivalesque, implying a bizarro world – a world so upside-down that "normies" need to walk a certain absurdist way to get along in the underworld, to navigate its dark corridors in disguise and to use this comic act of blending in to get what they came for and then get out again.

The classic retelling of this joke occurs in Mel Brooks's film *Young Frankenstein*. To get the joke, you need to know its horror-film context and conventions – originally a work of gothic science fiction, it was reworked into a series of horror films from the 1930s to 1950s, which were then much-parodied in the 1960s and 1970s. It goes like this: the mad scientist's henchman, Igor, is hunchbacked, limping and either clutches a withered arm to his chest or allows his semi-detached arm to swing as heavy as a sledgehammer beside him. Maybe both. To say that a person living in such a body would have mobility issues is an understatement. When the joke appears in *Young Frankenstein*, Marty Feldman pronounces his character's name Igor as "Eye-gor," a not-so-subtle pun on British comedian Feldman's enlarged eyes (a result of a thyroid disease called Graves' ophthalmopathy). The henchman character is often portrayed in the horror films of the 1930s and 1940s as being semi-verbal, communicating in grunts and moans – think of Eugene Levy's character Bruno in the parody "Monster Chiller Horror Theatre" on *SCTV* in the 1970s. But in Brooks's version, as played by Feldman, the hunchback is articulate and chatty as a schoolgirl. When Igor directs Gene Wilder's Dr. Frankenstein down a dark hall, Igor flings his cloak back over his hump, pulls a foreshortened cane from beneath his cloak and uses the cane to hobble down a short set of stairs, saying, "Walk this way." When Frankenstein begins to follow, Igor stops him by handing him the tiny cane, saying, "THIS way," indicating that Frankenstein must bend over to hobble forward on the short cane. Feldman claimed that he enacted the old joke as a goof on set and that Wilder, knowing the joke, followed through, but they hadn't intended for the sequence to make it to the final cut. Both Feldman and Wilder apparently protested when Mel Brooks declared it perfect for the tone of the comedy. Later, Feldman said that Brooks was right to keep it in the film.

I saw *Young Frankenstein* three times in the theatre in winter and spring of 1975. My walk, at the time, was a bit odd, but that was adolescence. We all still had vinegar bones and rubbery tendons, beginning to be flushed with hormones. My walk was still in formation. It still had flux capacity.

There's another story that claims that Steven Tyler of Aerosmith wrote the lyrics to "Walk This Way" after seeing *Young Franken-stein*. I've got all kinds of questions about that. Why does the protagonist take the girl's advice to "walk this way"? I know that he means direction; it's a come-hither phrase, and the girl seductively entices him to follow her. But, as the story goes, if Tyler wrote the lyrics after seeing *Young Frankenstein* and laughing with his bandmates about the joke, maybe the film is not so much an influence as an implication, emblematic of the work a phrase does when transferred to another context. Do the words *walk this way* in the song also imply manner? In what way does the girl teach him to walk? If the song is about her sexy walk, then is he supposed to walk the same way? (Tyler is also famous for singing "Dude Looks Like a Lady," so maybe Dude Walks Like a Lady.) And what note was Tyler meant to hit in that classic rock scream? I know, I know, it's a scream of desire, but it's hard not to also hear it as a scream of pain, one that is repeated so many times in the song that we have lots of chances to interpret it.

*

Not too long ago, I was giving a reading when a woman came out of the crowd and asked if I was *that* Tanis MacDonald. Turns out I was. She identified herself as a friend of a friend, someone I knew a little in my undergraduate years. She fired off a series of questions about my life ("Where do you live? Why there? What are you doing? Kids? Partner? So this is your book, eh?") and then she said, "I knew it was you by your walk." I didn't say anything about that, but I asked about her life, which she summed up in an unpunctuated rush: "Oh thirty years what's to tell I married X we got divorced I came out I started a business." *Right*, I thought, *what's to say about marriage or discovering you're queer or starting a business? But my walk – now that's a perennial topic.*

Recognizing me from my walk is easy to do, though I wondered why my old acquaintance thought my walk was more recognizable than my name or face. I wondered, too, why she thought it was a good thing to say that my geeky, lopey, gimpy turnout was the thing she remembered most about me after three decades. But I know – because I do it too – that people blurt out the truth in awkward social situations, making them even more awkward and more stringently social.

*

It's 1970, and I am in a Highland dance class at the community centre. Some of the older girls are amazing dancers and I especially admire the way one girl pounds the floor when she lands. She gets a lot of air when she jumps, her legs and arms precise and graceful. Her crisp *thuds* when she lands seem to be part of that: a drumbeat rhythm, the sound of a gallop. I am in the beginners' class, learning arm and toe positions. I don't thud rhythmically because I don't get to jump – yet. The instructor tells me to turn out my feet from the hips. This is a direction I will hear in every dance class I take for the rest of my life, be it jazz, ballet, modern. *Turn out from the hips. Dance this way.* I know that my teachers, more than once, looked at my elongated legs and neck and torso, and said some version of "This body should work better than it does." Dance instructors used to look at me like I was a machine that needed tuning. Tighten this screw or oil that cog.

I don't know the reason why my feet splay as they do. I can't blame the teenaged Highland dance instructor because I remember thinking, when I looked down at my eight-year-old feet, "This is easy. My feet already turn out." From inside my body, I was as surprised by what I could do as what I could not. Now that I can't dance, physical dexterity occupies a large chunk of my psyche as an impulse that lives on in my remembered body – the body that can still do everything, the body with its long legs that can kick over my head and do the splits. That remembered body is still real to me because I lived in it for so many years. So I am always surprised when my leg is stiff. It is an estranging experience and the thought that this is not my body occurs to me regularly. If I am not in my body, the body to which I am accustomed, where is that body? Does someone else have it? Suddenly, those body-switching plots of silly 1990s movies make a surreal and jolting sense: What am I doing in here?

But this is no movie; this is my body.

I have had degenerative disc disease for more than a decade, diagnosed only when my sciatica drove me to the doctor for X-rays. If you see me on an average day, you won't be able to tell. I can still walk a few kilometres at a time. I stand reasonably straight. But I don't wear heels of any kind, I don't carry any bag heavy enough to pull me to one side and I am just a little in love with my orthotics. I still love to walk. A day spent strolling through a neighbourhood in a new or beloved city, to take in its trees and sidewalks, stores and gardens, public squares and private houses, is a good day. A morning spent hiking a wooded trail or riverbank is also a favourite thing to do, even when I pay for it later. Which I always do.

My problems with footwear became neighbourhood knowledge when I walked home during the first week of grade three carrying my new shoes in my hands, bloody spots staining the toes and heels of my white tights. My friend's mother watched me pass her house and phoned ahead to my mother, who met me at our door a block later. Thereafter she always said at the shoe store, "Now be sure. I don't want to see you walking home in your stocking feet." I could never be sure of shoes and so I learned to walk with pain, to walk with blisters and scars, sometimes bulbous, sometimes bloody. The moment in the original "The Little Mermaid" story when she gains a pair of legs but pays with the sensation of knives slicing into her feet with every step, that was my life in shoes.

In recent years, however, I have learned to tell shoe store clerks that I am a traumatized shoe buyer. The smart ones know what I mean. I slip new shoes on my feet after consulting with the sales clerk and suddenly I have the weird sensation of not-pain. I try on a second pair and now I have another problem – I can't tell the difference between the pairs of shoes, between one way of not having foot pain and another. I buy the brightest ones.

*

"Stop walking like that," said an instructor at theatre school, "or you'll be crippled by the time you're forty." Rumour had it that this instructor had worked as the screen double for a particular glamorous and world-famous actress, and she would smile the smile of a cat with cream whenever anyone remarked on the cultivated resemblance. But she wasn't smiling now. She pointed to my feet: "Stand properly." I thought of her years later when sciatica started to slow me down, wondering if she had called down vengeful theatre gods on me. Other acting students were full of hopeful stories, how they had heard through a friend of a friend of their cousin who was an agent in New York about an actor who had completely changed their body to land a role. Every time a story like this was recounted, the teller's eyes would shine with hope. I could barely look at them. I never believed these stories of transformation, especially since they seemed to be recited most fervently by people who were never specific about what exactly they wanted to change about their bodies.

I could not hope for such a miracle because everyone was eager to name what it was I needed to change. In fact, some were eager to enact it. In one acting class, the instructor told us to choose a classmate and work up an accurate imitation of their walk to be performed in front of our fifteen-person class. I knew that a few people would choose me, but I was shocked when close to half the class did so. I was forced to sit in the studio, watching person after person get up, jut their feet to the side and galumph around the room. Some of these imitations were bad – not every person in that class was good at thinking themselves into another body. Some featured a glazed look in the eyes of the imitator, as if stunned. Some were pretty much perfect, in my estimation. All were exercises in humiliation that the instructor pretended were ripe with pedagogical opportunity. I did the exercise too, as it was a required assignment and I wasn't smart enough to figure out a way to say no. I don't remember who I imitated. The irony was enormous: How could I, with my distinctive walk, possibly make it appear like anyone else's? And how could I participate in this public body shaming?

*

One morning in September 2011, I got out of bed and felt a pain above my right hip. I touched it and stifled a gasp – it was like being prodded with a hot poker. In the following days, the hot-poker feeling spread down my back to my right buttock and wrapped like a python around to the front of my thigh. On the worst days, it ended mid-calf. Lying down was more painful than sitting up. There were times when the pain moved to the back of my mind, or I was able to concentrate on something else, but neither was a cure. I wasn't "getting better." They call it *sciatica*, which is late Middle English from the Late Latin *sciatica*, which itself is from the earlier Greek *iskhiadikos*, meaning "pain in the hips." The form is feminine. My limp is gendered.

In his *Philosophical Investigations*, Ludwig Wittgenstein noted the impossibility of describing pain, not only because it is so subjective but also because pain is a private language. Pain scales – widely used by the medical profession from the 1960s onward, with the intention of assisting patients in identifying their pain levels – suggest common terms for that private language. Some scales use facial expressions, some verbal descriptors and some colours. My favourite is the McGill Pain Index, which ranks chronic back pain as worse than phantom limb pain. How do the researchers know that? Given the impossibility of describing pain, how do pain researchers know anything? I'm fascinated by these scales because I find them impossible to use. And yet I chafe against agreeing with Wittgenstein. Is pain a completely private language? Or is it just a language that not everyone speaks? This tweet from Aaron Ansuini probes the painful mystery of living in a human body, in what could be an update of C.S. Lewis's *The Screwtape Letters*:

> *demon tries to inhabit my body*
> Demon: OUCH
> Me: yeah . . .
> Demon: WHAT THE HELL
> Me: I know
> Demon: EVERYTHING HURTS, WHY?? AND WHATS WRONG WITH THIS SHOULDER???
> Me: idk man, can I offer you a mint?

Ansuini is dead on. Wormwood, it hurts to be human. The mints are in a dish by the door. See yourself out.

*

In the snow, I can always spot my own footprints. Everyone else's footprints move in a straight line; mine make a herringbone pattern. I broke my left distal fibula in December 2012, and it was late January and still snowy by the time I was freed of my cast. I drove to the store and parked the car, went in, made my purchase and was on the way back through the light snow when I saw my own footprints – my left foot was leaving nearly straight footprints in the snow. *It's the cure*, I thought. *All I have to do is break the other leg!* But my straight-walking days didn't last. The fibula is too small a bone to resist the force of my leg's lifelong turnout. Soon my feet reasserted their old pattern. Hello, herringbone.

*

When you see me walk, you'll probably won't see much, especially if it's a good day. Maybe a little hitch from stiffness in my hip or a twinge in my ankle. My feet will be turned out, as they have been for my whole life, but you may not notice. With the odd walk come odd problems: blisters, calluses, ingrown toenails – it's kind of a mess down there.

But sometimes there's a weird hope. My friend Leena was watching the 2006 film *The Queen* and alerted me to Helen Mirren's walk as Queen Elizabeth: a pronounced turnout with a businesslike strut. "That's you," Leena said. The turnout is most evident in a scene when Mirren as the Queen invites Michael Sheen as Tony Blair to go for a walk as they discuss matters of state. Mirren rises and her feet, in sensible black pumps, turn out; she struts forward, saying briskly, "Are you a walker?" This walk, as performed by Mirren, is both surprising and completely right. She declares, "I think best on my feet." For the record, none of the videos I found of the real Queen Elizabeth shows this turnout; in real life, her feet go straight. But that doesn't matter; Mirren's Oscar-winning choice to "walk this way" demonstrated, for me, a sisterhood of the splay-foot.

Many of us have been fed a steady diet of body-as-machine or body-as-flesh-puppet metaphors and live in a perpetual low-level state of confusion with respect to how our machines/puppets actually work. We are unlicensed operators. If your body isn't broken, don't fix it, and above all don't think about it. If it is broken, you will be encouraged to not talk about it, for almost mystical reasons: to name the devil is to invite him into your house. But you will be able to see material evidence of bodies in crisis; you will be able to recognize people by their physical manifestations of pain or bones that have grown a certain way. And you will be able to call attention to those in public, if you will, via imitation or just by saying, "I recognized you by your walk."

Encouraged by the Ministry of Silly Walks, the cottage industry in imitating other people's walks must be large, for so many seem comfortable doing it. A colleague who I like and respect asked about my broken leg via ellipsis and action, saying, "How's your . . .?" then imitating a dead leg that he dragged behind him. This imitation set up a logical contradiction. My limp is fine; it's present and accounted for. My leg, on the other hand, resists articulation. My limp persists, even when you can't see it. My limp is bigger than the leg it uses. My limp is there especially when you can't see it. My limp is prosthetic to the idea of a leg, supplementary to walking.

Walk this way, says Marty Feldman.

Walk this way, says Steven Tyler.

Walk this way, said my grade eight geography teacher. He asked us to push our desks aside to create a wide aisle down the middle of the room and then showed us how to walk. He described and then demonstrated how we should walk – young men first and then young women. It's hard for me to recall what he prescribed for the boys as that advice was completely overshadowed by his demonstration of how women walk. He didn't mince or simper; he didn't prance or giggle. He started at one end of the room and glided across it like old Hollywood glamour. He moved like Harlow through Monte Carlo. He attributed to us not only a degree of grace and coordination that none of us had at thirteen, but also the breasts and hips most of us had not yet grown. He instructed us then to put our desks back and he never referred to it again. From older siblings, we learned that he taught this lesson every year.

This was an exercise in gender prescription, no question, and I am torn between thinking of the demonstration – its seriousness, its unusualness, its annual repetition – and contemplating its legacy. Thirteen-year-olds are inundated with people telling them what to do, admonitions against some behaviours and praise for others, and I am struck that the geography teacher didn't mock us, or parody us, or shout directions at us. It seems as though he took the problems of our bodies seriously and offered a serious answer. No doubt his answer was limited – in gender, in style, in aspect – but it was an answer offered more thoughtfully than most answers to such impossible questions. The question he tried to answer was not "How do I walk?" but what we wanted to know but could not ask: "How can I be in the world?" and "What happens if my body doesn't fit in the world?" His answer may have been "Walk this way because it will help you fly under the radar, walk this way to wear a mask that will protect you until it's safe to walk any damn way you please." He put his own body on the line to answer what we could not and would never ask.

Have I mentioned that he was short, stocky and wore the same two poly-blend suits day in and day out? That he taught us this class a year after *Young Frankenstein* came out? That he had a British accent and a glass eye? Truth is not only stranger than fiction; it is endlessly repetitive.

Walk this way, said my friend who made a living as a female impersonator.

Walk this way, said my mother who never learned to drive; who had a chunk of skin on her left shin removed in 1964 due to melanoma but never, ever limped.

*

The video of Run-DMC's 1986 cover of Steven Tyler and Joe Perry's "Walk This Way" features duelling versions of the song performed by Aerosmith and Run-DMC, including Tyler demonstrating a prancing "walk" during the song. When Joseph Simmons and Darryl McDaniels of Run-DMC join Aerosmith on stage, the three singers perform a "walk" together: part line dance, part strut.

To be recognizable for one's manner of personal locomotion is curious: a standout silhouette, a distinct gait, a way of standing. Caught between one prescription for my glasses and a stronger one that is inevitably coming my way, I can sometimes recognize people from a distance and sometimes not. This is usually not a problem except when someone waves or gestures in my direction and I think, "Do I know them?" I like it when I can see someone from a distance and have that second of recognition, something small but definite. So I can read someone by how they stand. So I can tell them by their walk – the way people tell me from my walk, my gendered limp, my splay-foot stance, my prosthetic pain that supplements my leg as more than a leg.

I checked the sheet music – the rock scream of "Walk This Way" hits a high C. My hip registers that high note on good days and on bad, part limp, part strut. I recognize you: walk this way.

This Limp Goes to Eleven

I
Among the pretty
elbows and Cuban heels,
the only thing moving: galumph.

II
I am of slow leg,
infantry
in an analgesic war.

III
If ontogeny recapitulates phylogeny, then Darwin
owes me a new hip and a twenty-minute head start.

IV
Many have tried to
straighten me to fly
right, but crooked is
as crooked tries.

V
If you walk this miracle mile
with me, I promise we'll be
right as Ripley. My limp's a stiff
joke: I do not know if it's
with me or at me.

VI
My little mermaid feet stab
the stairs, pinwheels whir
above my head. The glass in
my right hip is sciatica
shattered like Attica.
To ask after me is
to act me out.

VII
Call me Ahab. The plot
of the limp is a constant
search for prosthesis.
A good apparatus is
hard to find.

VIII
My walking wound takes
all day. There's no telling
who's history in the faking.
I know Long John Silver takes
no wasted steps.

IX
(You're too polite to notice,
but crawling gives me
the most distracting rug burn.)

X
Grin and bear with
me. I must be
out of your mind.

XI
I can't dance; don't
task me. To act me out
is to drag. Under
the same stars, they
shoot horses.

She's Got Legs

My Mother Walks

My mother never learned to drive, so she and I walked everywhere. She grew up in rural Manitoba with four older brothers, and of course one of them tried to teach her to drive, but she said it always went wrong. She'd be driving along on the gravel road with her brother beside her and he'd say, "Hey, look at that," or something else that drew her attention to the field beside her. Before she knew it, the car would be heading into the field. This is a common mistake for learners, and we all learn not to turn the wheel just because we turn our heads. After I had my driver's licence for a year, I offered to teach her, but she said no, she preferred me to drive her around or to walk. And that was that.

I used to have dreams in which some disaster occurred and my mother HAD to drive. These dreams were always accompanied by the sight of her pulling up to the curb and parking, then getting out of the car like nothing was unusual. In the dream, I always remarked on this amazing hidden ability, and she would shrug and say, "Oh, I can do it if there's an emergency."

But for all of my childhood and well beyond, she and I walked to the grocery store, to the bus, to the dentist, to the library, to my grandmother's place and to church and back. I walked to school and back, to the baseball field and back, to the skating rink and back and to my friends' houses. We owned a car, but it was for "special occasions" according to my father, who also took the bus to work every day. I would sometimes walk to meet my dad as he got off the bus after work. Until I was sixteen and learned to drive, it never occurred to me that it could be otherwise.

When I was very young, my mother called me "a good little walker," which I assumed was the highest and most mature form of praise. I scorned kids who whined after a block's walk. Part of the compliment was rooted in the fact that my mother was very grateful I could walk at all. I was ill for several months as a toddler, and the pediatrician who examined me told my mother that he would get some tests done, but he was concerned I may have rheumatic fever. Medical thought at the time advised that the typical kind of kinetic toddler movement would strain and perhaps permanently damage my overtaxed heart. The doctor, with his broad Highland accent, lectured my mother the way only an old white man could, with some strange special frisson to his words – he knew one of her older brothers and therefore always addressed her by her maiden name as if he were an army sergeant and she a new recruit. "For the love of God," he said, "don't let that child take a step on her own. You carry her." So I was carried everywhere, or as my mother put it, "Your feet never touched the floor." All the photo evidence from that time shows me in the arms of my father, my mother, my aunts or my grandmother. This lasted until I was about three, when the Scottish doctor lifted the decree and I was allowed to run around as much as I liked. A more reliable test for rheumatic fever became available shortly after, and it was determined that I had never had it. But in a true example of "better safe than sorry," I was duly hoisted and tucked under someone's arm for several months.

When I was hospitalized in my twenties for the removal of a benign but aggressive spinal tumour, the nurses would smile when they took my vitals, and more than one remarked that they loved to hear a healthy heart. My mother would grin by my bedside. I know she claimed my healthy heart as her private achievement, the part of me she preserved by carrying me around all of those months, even though the disease she dreaded never actually touched me. But it was more complicated than that; she herself had survived a malignant melanoma on her right shin about a year before my rheumatic fever scare. To remove the melanoma, the surgeon sketched out a rectangle of skin surrounding it and cut to the bone – a six-by-four-inch excavation that remained visible on my mother's leg for the rest of her life. She underwent an early form of chemotherapy that involved being dosed with a chemical derivative of mustard gas. It made her grossly, violently ill for weeks, but it worked.

From Mary Karr's memoir *The Liars' Club*: "The doctors piped mustard gas through Grandma's leg to try to stop the spread of her melanoma . . . Today it's hard to imagine a treatment more medieval." It's hard to imagine, full stop. I thought my mother might be misremembering until I checked up on the history of mustard gas as chemotherapy and found out it was true. This was years before I read Karr's book so my doubt was more because I'd never heard any other anecdotes about this treatment, only my mother's. The scar was just part of her leg, and later, evidence of survival. As a child, I was allowed to gently touch the excavated spot if I asked first. It was smooth and had the consistency of melted-then-dried wax. My mother survived the mustard gas treatment, but Karr's grandmother did not.

I never heard her discuss how she began to walk again on that traumatized leg, the leg that survived and did not have to be removed but which she would need to protect from infection for years to come. So she, too, was newly returned to walking by the time the doctor told her to carry me everywhere.

We never referred to my mother as disabled; I can hear her now, scoffing at the word. She had a brother who lost a leg in battle in

France and wore a prosthetic. She might have considered him disabled, though I suspect not. But she always wore pants and never dresses, except for the floor-length hostess gowns that were popular in the seventies. When I was ten, my first baseball coach was an athletic woman who was also the mother of a school friend; I knew about women athletes, but it was her motherhood that threw me. Embarrassingly long for a future feminist, I puzzled over how a coach could be a mother, and how a mother could be a coach. My coach had a pitching arm like a cannon and she batted pop flies to us for hours. Meanwhile my mother couldn't even run for the bus.

When I got older and moved to another city, on my visits home, my mother and I developed a habit of walking while we figured things out: elaborate meals and trips and parties, solutions to money problems and the pact between us as women who solved things, who got things done. We did this when I drove her somewhere too, but walking was always more fruitful, more philosophical, more inventive. The action of walking made us more determined to make a plan work. It was our alone time, a time for confidences. My mother and I were walking when I told her that a neighbour had made a weird and creepy pass at me. We were walking when we planned for her to visit me, wrestling with her fear of flying. My mother sometimes saved hard questions for our walks. When my cousin was diagnosed with schizophrenia, my mom wanted to know what it was and how it could be treated and what caused it, and she waited for a walk to ask me. For this conversation and many others, I had to tell her that her confidence was misplaced, that I didn't know about every subject in the world, that her guess was a good as mine. "I'll look it up when we get home," I'd say, and that was good enough for her.

My mother walked alone and with my father. While he was in hospital in November 2004, she fell on the ice on her way back from the hairdresser. She had gone to get her hair done so she'd look nice when visiting my dad – this was shortly after his second operation to remove the cancer spreading through his digestive organs. She was hurrying home to get all the treats she had assembled to tempt my father's appetite – his favourite biscuits and cheese, ginger cookies, slices of lemon loaf – when she slipped and found herself suddenly lying in the middle of an intersection between a busy thoroughfare and a side street. A car stopped and a woman leapt out, asking if she was all right. "Yes," my mother said, "but I've got to get to the hospital." The woman answered, "I'll take you there right now." "No, wait," my mother said, "I need the cookies!" She directed her good Samaritan back to the house, gave this kind stranger the keys so that she could run inside and collect the bag of treats, and then and only then my mother consented to be driven to the hospital. She was examined in Emergency, diagnosed as bruised and shaken up but otherwise okay, and put in a wheelchair so she could go upstairs to see my dad. "Oh, we laughed when I was wheeled into the room!" she told me later.

I was not laughing. A mere seventy-two hours after my mother's fall, my dad died. His heart gave out after that second operation.

I flew home. By that point, my mother couldn't walk without a walker and I have no memory of how we got her from the car to the church for the service, and back home. Carefully, I guess. When the funeral was over and it was just my mom and me again, she told me that she couldn't stay dependent on the walker, that she needed to start walking without it. We started practising in the hallway, where it was carpeted and there were no obstacles. I put my hands out toward her, palms up, and she gripped my wrists and took one shaky step, then another. "I'm afraid of falling," she said. "I've got you," I assured her. We made a circuit of the house, inch by inch. After a few days, I removed my hands and asked her to walk toward me. I felt like the meanest physical therapist alive when she looked up at me and said, "I can't do it." My mother had the bluest eyes in the world, and they were even paler when they swam with tears.

Reader, she did it. Step by step, until she was steady on her feet and gaining strength. She remained afraid of falling, and so began a decade-long battle with staying mobile and safe during icy prairie winters. She bought what she called "my spikes" – rubber and metal crampons that slipped onto regular boots – and she wore them everywhere in the winter. She could have had her groceries delivered, but she preferred to walk to the grocery store, wearing her spikes and hauling her handcart. She walked forty-five minutes to church every Sunday, giving herself enough time to get there without rushing the three and a half kilometres. On very cold or blizzardy days, she'd accept a ride from a fellow congregant, but otherwise she would walk. I told her that cabs were relatively cheap and better to use when she had to carry things. I told her that people wanted to assist her, that any number of folks would drive her if she asked. But she only shook her head. Walking was independence. If she could do that, she could do anything.

The final spring of her life, my mother's neighbour found her sitting on the steps of her back porch, a little dizzy from the hot walk home from church. He helped her to her feet and she said, "Oh, Sandy, it's you!" as though her power of recognition only kicked in when she was on her feet. But it was the beginning of the end. She couldn't find her balance getting up from a chair. Her eyes didn't quite focus. She mistook me for her sister, her long-dead mother and once for my father, himself dead for eleven years. She had fallen twice and her back was giving her a great deal of pain. I got her to the hospital, where they took X-rays and ran tests and could not figure out what was wrong.

As days passed, every medical professional who entered her room wanted to spend more time with my mother's right shin. They were obsessed by the old, massive scar, a welcome and fascinating distraction from the woman in the bed who could not stand or walk, who was weakening by the day for reasons they couldn't discover.

If they couldn't treat what was killing her, they would at least be passionately curious about what hadn't killed her. They were young scientists of the human body, and most wouldn't have seen an epidermal excavation like hers. Maybe it was even an object of corridor gossip. But when one young man saw the scar and gasped, "Wow, when did THIS happen?" I snapped, "In 1963."

Time passes, and sometimes we come to know those we lost better after they're gone than we did during their fraught final days. I know my mother would never have called herself a feminist, or an athlete, or a community leader. But she was all of those things. She'd say to me as we left the shopping centre, with supper to put on and my father due home in thirty minutes, "It's time to pick 'em up and put 'em down." And we'd stride with purpose.

Ricochet

An Arcade

The walk is in the raising of the foot as in the laying of it down.
    – Rabindranath Tagore, *Stray Birds*

Found preserved in cooled volcanic ground on a savannah: the dark afterplaster of wet ash, the goo of lava hardened to evidence, a woman walking. Lucy, our mother of bipedalism, she who tipped back onto her heels and whistled upright, far-seeing, the horizon now hers to amble toward. Those small footprints – heel, then arch, then toe, then heel. Perpetual stepping machine. You picked a fine time to walk here, Lucille. Lucy's knees learned to lock. Her ankles were Pliny's promise of something new out of Africa, Mitochondrial Eve stepping out.

*

I am walking, and the catcalls have fallen far behind me, the car of drunken man-boys screaming "CUNT!" at me or at all of the women on the sidewalk that day, that month, that year. All of us looked up and looked at and past each other: *Was that meant for her, or her, or me?* I am walking with the bark of my sciatica, my snapping snarling fascia, my degenerating discs, my swollen ankle, my child-bearing hips, my slippery pelvic floor, my stuttering menopause, my Body Misogyny Index.

*

Left ankle rattles and hip shrieks. I pass a man who darts into the underbrush, and I wonder if I should walk back the way I came. I watch for loose stones and birds and mushrooms and dogs and deer and men walking alone or walking together. I calculate odds and risks and percentages. I am Rosalind Franklin measuring the density of DNA on a helical twist in the path. I am Katherine Johnson mapping rocket trajectories and a safe route home. I am Ada Lovelace. I am the difference engine.

I walk in ugly shoes, jet-fuelled by the racing thoughts of a thousand women who can't leave the house or tread these sidewalks without being taunted, raped, killed. I walk into my rage like heading into a night forest, carrying incandescent heat in my rib cage. I swing my rage like a lantern and open its cage so a single beam sweeps the grass and leaves, and the birds say, "Oh, it's you in your pain and your flaring walk through walk through."

*

A woman walking on her two legs is like a dog preaching; that it is done at all prompts howling.

*

To the author of the fiction craft book who wrote this prompt for beginners, "Write a short story from the point of view of a young girl being pursued through a dark park by a crazed man with a knife," fuck off.

To the same author who followed up with, "Now rewrite it from the point of view of the man with a knife," fuck off again.

You left *crazed* off the second description, like he's just a guy, could be anyone; like he needs our understanding – hey you know, why don't we look at this from his point of view?

Do these deserve to be compared like sugar or salt, like striped or spotted?

Right now, I have all the words. But you don't have to accept that. You can revise at your leisure, as soon as I leave the room. I'll send in a woman with a knife.

I know that's not fair. Oh, here she is.

*

Stride like a giraffe, then bounce like Yogi Bear. Limp like a quarterback, a geriatric hitch, a flat-foot shuffle. Never plan a route but ricochet off faint trails and wide fields. St. Francis guards a back gate by a stormwater pond and no one picks the wild crabapples there. The city mows down yarrow on the verge. Let lost cat posters become desire lines. In August, the Anglican Church sign still reads "He is Risen!" A neighbour changes her backyard flag each day.

Found: T. Rex beneath a pine, bigger than the cones, turquoise with brown stripes and forehead. Moulded lizard, queen of plastic. She's stomped her way out here to the playground; she means business. In my pocket, she kicks like a rabbit. I'll take her back when the snow melts. She crouches on my desk. Her tiny eye follows me everywhere, mouth open in a roar or an aria.

*

A couple walks toward me on the road in the conservation area. If there had been traffic, I would have been walking against it. Thanks, Elmer the Safety Elephant. No traffic: sun, trees, three people.

Then in a flash of fur and muscle, something sinuous slips from the woman's hands and slides into her red quilted bag. A long lean spine curves and then is gone. The couple walks mid-road but moves aside to let me pass. The bag bulges and shifts in her arms.

*

Women walked away from Hiroshima and Nagasaki, from the Donner Party, from Wounded Knee, from dust bowl farms in the thirties, from the Holodomor, from jackboots and from his belt and his fists and the legal marital rape that kept her pregnant.

Sometimes there is only staying. Sometimes there is living through it.

The forced marches; the carrying of jugs of water or grain; the five miles to town and five miles back in the dead of winter; the walk to the bus at midnight or later, baby strapped to her back or front; the long walk to where the government sent her, soldiers riding alongside; the dotted line on the highway where people speed up in their trucks to scare the women walking.

The most dangerous one hundred feet I've walked was out the front door and down the sidewalk.

*

If she walks by, you'll know. She'll walk the long way and make it look short. Her scissor legs cut paper. She can walk it off and walk it back on again. She's got a walk that would stop a clock. Relationship goals: find someone who looks at you the way she looks at the horizon.

*

How far did Harriet Tubman walk in a day and a night, in her whole life, over hills, across borders, under trees? A young woman walking in the dark through places where people would kill her for walking, for the hundred-dollar reward, for the hell of it. Ninety miles between Dorchester, Maryland and Philadelphia, along the Choptank River into Delaware, through headaches and blackouts, dizzy spells, carrying a gun. Her stride a unit of measurement: walk seventy Tubmans down the road and turn left at the willow. Thirteen round trips, thirty years waiting for a veteran's pension. Walking with corns and bunions and blisters, toenails bruised and falling off. Eight thousand kilometres and counting.

*

I have two legs to stand on, and both hurt. I could get a hip replacement, titanium and plastic with ball bearing and socket wrench – this must be the joint! My leg licks flames down my knee, a long loose leak; my calves are drunk without alcohol, dipsomaniac ankles, self-brewing thighs. Anaconda of the sartorius, a muscled rope. Everyone thinks their own dreams of flying are the most elegant. The sirens sing of knowledge, and they'll make me walk for it.

I'm so hip it hurts. Long the figure and ground of the step, that damp ball of femur in the catcher's mitt of the acetabulum, socket set to the stars, backed by the turkey fantail of the gluteus minimus. Is this the place that launched a thousand hips and burned the topless towers on the Crest of Ilium? Perambulation's a pyrrhic victory, winning at walking at cost, at best. At worst, I am dragged behind a chariot, prisoner of piriformis, that flattened pyramid of muscles woven like a rush mat, clenched like a fist. Turns me into Samson, grinding my own bone in the mill of the walk. Wittgenstein was wrong: When Hecuba barks like a dog, I understand every word.

*

If you are walking and your friend calls you, sit under a tree and talk to her. Feel the bark on your back and the dust on your legs. Feel fifteen again. Repetition is love. Fox prints don't look like dog prints. Sameness becomes newness begets oldness begins likeness. Like the river.

*

The game is five-toed hike, paces wild. I see your right foot, and I raise you my left. I was raised to be a riser. Lay down your boot and your sword; lay them down like they are twin six-month-olds you just got to sleep. Lay them down like fainters caught in your arms as their knees buckled.

This is so pedestrian. My toes are so hammered. My corns are so on the cob. My heels are so high on life, so low on the bucket list. We are the limpers, the ambulatory lame, old injuries kicking us when it's cold or damp, or when the Sphinx ravages our city and everyone thinks we've got the answers.

Just Walk Away, Renée

*

If
it
is solved
by walking,
how then to reclaim
the paradox of motion as
an ancient female history of unreality
since some declare that Diogenes the cynic came
closest when he stood up and walked
away and we know
a woman
went
first.
∧

Seeing Through the Rain

A Ghost Walk

It rained for hours the day of my unofficial feminist walking tour of Toronto's Annex district, a walk I had planned in part to consider the authority of my own walking body. Though the weather was wet, my plan was simple: I wanted to see a couple of monuments – mostly to do with Toronto's female writers – that had been established after I left the city for points west. I was looking for three places that memorialized women whose writing was important to me: Gwendolyn MacEwen Park, the Jane Jacobs roseway and Jay Macpherson Green. There were other places on the way that I wanted to look out for as well, places where I had walked regularly when I was a young person who walked the city for hours a day – a life that I just don't lead anymore.

Toronto changes fast. In a way, the city where I lived for more than a decade no longer exists, but in other ways it is always there, just beneath the surface: memory, traces, history, layers of urban life. There was also an agenda that I had hidden from myself: I wanted my younger eyes back, just for a few hours. I wanted, in some ways, to ghost myself, to be there and not be there, to memorialize while remaining unseen. The rain, then, was a perfect cover.

I passed the 5.7-metre-tall water jug in Taddle Creek Park, a sculpture known as *The Vessel* by Ilan Sandler. The sculpture operates both as a fountain and as cistern storage for water used to irrigate the park. It commemorates Taddle Creek, one of the many creeks in an extensive watershed system diverted to flow underneath Toronto's streets. According to Sandler's website, *The Vessel* was designed to overflow so that the sound of the water falling to the pavement would drown out the sound of traffic. The rain was doing that already, and the overfull vessel spilled lavishly, another form of rain.

*

In Maureen Hynes's collection *Sotto Voce* there is a pair of poems titled "Are you ladies lost?" prompted by men seeing Hynes and her wife looking up into a tree at a first-of-season (or out-of-season) robin in February. The use of the term *ladies* suggests just what Elizabeth Wilson writes in *The Sphinx in the City* – that the two people (female, queer, married, nature-aware) must be read via the social conventions of "ladies" (elderly or otherwise unfit to be outdoors, non-athletic, unused to the route, addled) in order for the city to maintain order. But the gaze of the two women looking steadily up into the tree disrupts the order and suggests something better, what Wilson calls the "pleasurable chaos" of city life.

As chaos goes, stopping to look at a detail of one's environment seems minor, but it is surprisingly disruptive, depending on what body you occupy and where you are. In Hynes's "Are you ladies lost?," the title makes hay of the idea that two men step in to rescue the women with their knowledge; it is poised as a joke, for the women's knowledge has created the scene. This knowledge will go on to complete the poem, as the two women speculate about the robin's presence in February only to be met by "concern" from the two men, who don't offer a response about the robin or the women's question. In fact, they don't look at the tree even as the robin's "trilling song" saturates the air around them. Instead, they mention that the Canadian men's hockey team took gold at the Olympics the night before. "Our team," snorts Hynes's speaker, rich in irony; these men are not on "our team" ecologically, socially, sexually or ornithologically.

Kirby, via Patrick Califia, in *Poetry is Queer*: "Queer: a person who self-proclaims the authority of their own body in defiance of church and state."

If you walk, you transgress a space. You may or may not be welcome in this space, even if it's a public space, even if you are breaking no law. You also see things, people, places, and they see you. And if the politics of looking invite mansplaining, snarkiness and just plain misunderstanding, the politics of being seen are even snarlier. In public space, we are always seeing through the curtain of rain that is our ability (or lack of it) to control how we look, who sees us and how we wish to be seen. And sometimes, the active observer loses the ability to recognize this curtain of rain as a constant; sometimes I slip up and overstay, overlook. In the British city of Leeds, I once watched a bird for so long that a woman waiting at the bus stop demanded, "So, are you going to buy it?," gesturing to the house behind the tree. (If you really spend a lot of time looking, money MUST be involved.) Not two weeks later, on the same trip, a furious elderly woman in London barked at me as I followed a wood pigeon from tree to tree, "Do ye not have houses where you live?" She'd assumed I was staring at (or maybe even into) the homes alongside the trees. Staring is rude, but looking is subversive. Stopping and looking up can discomfit people. Sometimes it is not a happy thought to think that others can see more than you do. Sometimes looking makes me forget myself, in the best way possible, but travelling alone is a conduit to personal invisibility. The longer I spent in urban centres where I was just passing through, the more my sense of visibility was eroded.

The politics of being seen, and to be seen looking, are no joke. It matters who is doing the looking, and where. To be white and to stop and stare is intrusive but allowed. To be female and white, to stop and stare is to be either confused or covetous. To be Black, to stop and look intently can be dangerous. Ecologist J. Drew Lanham's "9 Rules for the Black Birdwatcher" skewers the unbearable whiteness of birdwatching. Lanham has been credited with alerting many white birders to the intrinsic racism of their obsession. As Lanham notes in *The Home Place*, "The chances of seeing someone who looks like me while on the trail are only slightly greater than those of sighting an ivory-billed woodpecker." The combination of humour and historical horror in Lanham's writing is not only a long-overdue dig at the mostly white, mostly male birder demographic but also a sustained critique of denatured, classist ideas of nature writing as an ahistorical, late-capitalist practice of acquisition that aligns chillingly with surveillance culture. To stop and look is to be looked at while looking, in the wild or on an urban street.

*

The monument in tiny Gwendolyn MacEwen Park is a cast sculpture of MacEwen's head on a plinth gazing serenely above and beyond. She looks timelessly youthful, as young as when she married Milton Acorn. She was a prodigy, to be sure, though for me, MacEwen is, always and forever, author of the poem "The Transparent Womb," in which she notes that the neighbourhood children wander through her house looking for fruit and enumerates her reasons for why she never had a child. The older MacEwen, living below the poverty line, was an Annex resident on and off.

The sculpture's mild expression both denies and confirms her as a complicated, brilliant, frustrating woman. She was the source for the character Isis in Margaret Atwood's short story "Isis in Darkness" and was commemorated in Linda Griffiths's play *Alien*

Creature. MacEwen's elusive literary persona was called "Shadow-maker" by Rosemary Sullivan in her biography of the same name, and it's the name that perhaps goes the furthest to capturing the essence of MacEwen's life and work. Because I never met MacEwen personally, I think a lot about how both she and I had lived in Toronto for years without crossing paths. I want desperately to find significance in it, but can't. It just loops around my brain and spins. I am alone as I stand staring up at her as she looks over my head, drizzle pinging off my eyelids, raindrops dripping from hers.

*

Are you ladies lost? Are you ladies? Are you?

In her second poem titled "Are you ladies lost?" Hynes riffs on what it is to be lost in the ecological disasters of the twenty-first century: "we do have a kind of science-fiction look on our faces / not lost / but perhaps losing." It is no coincidence that the next poem in the book is "Late Love Song, with an Orange: A Cento." This love poem includes the two women's romance and marriage, with erotic moments from their sex life, defying the solicitude of "are you ladies lost?" Additionally, the poem is a cento, a form that reuses lines from other writers to compose a new poem. "Late Love Song" is community written: "our team" of simpatico writers, birders, elders, queers and allies, and that "science fiction look" asks: When we are outside, can we be ourselves as we want to be?

Queer folks have long been associated with urban living and maker culture, and given that many LGBTQ+ folks move to urban spaces to find solidarity with others, that is a fair association. But I think too of queer writers who resist that easy equivalence: the writing of Ivan Coyote, and their lifelong and much-written love of semi-rural life in the Yukon; and Ali Blythe's desert landscapes in his book *Hymnswitch*. In an interview with Elaine Kahn in *The*

Creative Independent, writer Cody-Rose Clevidence talks about their off-grid life in the Arkansas Ozarks, and notes that their preference is either wilderness or teeming metropolis because both provide productive isolation and safety: "I think of New York City as kind of a wilderness, and then I also think of the actual wilderness as a wilderness, but any place that's not one of those two extremes is not somewhere that feels good for me."

The wilderness is not always a safe space for women, for people of colour, for the queer-identified. Trees have hidden beatings and murder as many times as they have hidden people from their tormentors. And I don't want to pretend that there's easy solidarity between these groups, though they are all well-acquainted with the affective push for solitude, for daring, for release from the social constructions of gender or race or sexuality, for a more elemental experience of time and place. When the norm is not your friend, the solitude of a wild space or a city where no one knows you can be.

*

There's a great moment in Janice Jo Lee's one-person play, *Will You Be My Friend*, in which the lead character, a twentysomething Korean Canadian woman who has just broken up with her oblivious white-dude boyfriend, resists her bestie's suggestion that they go for a walk with this dead-on racial characterization: "No, walking's too much like hiking, and that's all white people do." Lee is not wrong, and as it continues to pour and grow chillier by the block, I think about why I've chosen to spend my one day in the city in such an isolated pursuit of a personal mythology. The psychogeography of looking for these monuments to women I admire with the rain bucketing down feels like a punishing pilgrimage, neither walking nor hiking. Slogging? Mushing?

Soaked to the skin and walking west, I search for Jacobs' Ladder, the roseway planted in honour of Jane Jacobs. But on the way, I keep an eye out for two more personal sites: an apartment block where my sometimes-boyfriend used to live, and a former workplace in an Annex house with an office on the upper floor where I worked for eighteen months. I have the same problem with each place – I find the buildings, but I don't quite recognize them. The real buildings don't pulse or glow the way they do in my memory. The apartment building looks good, better than when I used to visit here in the 1980s. The trees around it have matured, and its stark modernist structure has softened with grime and age. The building looks less like a sleek container for urban living, and the steadily falling rain makes a scrim through which I can see its shabby beauty. When I find my former workplace, it's so small that I have trouble believing that four people could have fit inside let alone worked at four different desks in the upstairs office.

My desire to be a ghost on this walk, to haunt my younger self while visiting the ghosts of women I admired, isn't because I want to be absent from this plane of existence. I want to slip between now and then. I turn a corner and find Loretto College, a girls' private Catholic school, has been turned into condos. A Toronto friend first showed me the college in the early eighties, gesturing at its sprawling edifice as though I would know its history. Years later, I read that Anahareo (Gertrude Bernard), the Mohawk writer and conservationist, had been promised a year's tuition at the college's sister institution, Loretto Abbey – a boarder's school in North Toronto – and that she almost went, but she met an older guy at her summer job in Temagami in 1925 and followed Grey Owl (Archie Belaney) onto his trapline. I don't know what would have happened to Bernard, a young Mohawk woman, in a Catholic boarding school, but I'm betting it wouldn't have been good. There can, of course, be no monument to things that didn't happen, and the train of associations from condos to the college to the abbey to that young Mohawk woman who would write *Devil in Deerskins* is an imaginative fillip that spins in my head like a tiny whirlpool. Through the drizzle, I can see young couples through the windows of the new condos in the former college building, living in the monument that is not one, the bullet that Anahareo dodged.

With several blocks behind me and no one looking for or at me, I head to the monument to Jane Jacobs, the roseway in St. Alban's Square. The square itself is easy to find, but I walk its perimeter twice and can't find the monument or any signage pointing to it. The park seems more like a throughway, a greenish desire line fronting the imposing church (Cathedral of St. Alban the Martyr, no less) and schoolyard. I circle both, thinking maybe the roseway will be prominent alongside the public buildings, a monument for kids to note as they enter the building or play in the yard. Nope. Jacobs was a major thinker in the latter half of the twentieth century and into the twenty-first – someone whose ideas about livable cities are quoted internationally, and whose activism in stopping the Spadina Expressway in the 1980s made her an especially lively figure in Toronto. Where is her monument? I eventually find it, a tiny plaque hidden by roses, bolted to black iron fencing. The plaque reads only: "Jacobs' Ladder – This Roseway created by her neighbours is dedicated to JANE JACOBS and her vision of living cities. Grassroots Albany, 1997." I look for something more, a supplement or further signage, but there are none. If you live in Toronto and have never seen Jacobs' Ladder, I'm not surprised. Monuments are rarely large enough to satisfy my outsized imagination, and sometimes they aren't even enough for passersby to notice.

A block south of the nearly hidden roseway, in front of a vintage Annex-style house, are three enormous trees covered in vines and a small but well-polished, finely maintained sign noting the house as Jacobs' Toronto residence from 1971 to 2006. The current owners keep a garden that frames the sign but does not hide it. The distance between the two plaques is one city block. Hundreds of cities all over the world host a "Jane's Walk" each May. I start to think that the roseway is intentionally modest: citizen-planted, citizen-weeded, with a plaque that is covered not by design but because, as Jacobs might have said, it really is about the roses. The plaque is truly local knowledge – if you know, you know.

Holed up in a café on Bloor, eating an omelette and trying to dry out a bit, I think of how many writers, how many unplaced monuments are missing from my tour. One of the first book launches I attended was Lillian Allen's launch of *Women Do This Every Day* at the Poor Alex, just down the street and around the corner from Jacobs' house. That's where I would put a monument, though no one was asking me. Dionne Brand had lived in the Annex; so had Elizabeth Smart, Marian Engel and Catherine O'Hara, but there were no monuments to them, either. So I plot a circuitous route to the third point in my triangle: Jay Macpherson Green.

I detour to another personal (and coincidentally literary) site: the former home of playwright Tom Hendry, father to a high school friend and the first writer I knew in Toronto. I follow the route that I walked every time I visited, turning down their street and finding the house three-quarters of the way down the block. The Hendrys were very good to me; I ate dozens of dinners in that house, attended many parties and listened to thousands of hours of music while lounging around the third-floor bedrooms and rooftop balcony. I think I can find the house blindfolded until I see the street, which had hosted artsy-shabby older houses when I first saw it in 1980. I recall the house as being sizeable but unassuming on the outside, and subtly chic inside. The surrounding houses had been in varying degrees of decay and disrepair; lawns were shaggy, gardens a bit wild. It was not the suburbs. But that was before gentrification. Thirty years later, I stand on the opposite side of the street and try to pick out the former Hendry house, knowing that I can't rely on any removable or added features: windows, porches, dormers, awnings, paint colour. I look, mostly, for the third-floor window to the room with all the records. My memory stalled like a cold engine – I couldn't identify the house. My ghosting was getting a little too real.

I trudge to Avenue Road, rain fogging my glasses. I squint at Google Maps directions on my phone and walk north and then north some more. I am on the verge of giving up when I finally find Jay Macpherson Green, a bigger slice of land than MacEwen's tiny traffic island. And despite my disgruntled wandering around, it is better marked than Jacobs' Ladder. The green is a corner park by a bus stop, backed by a residential street, and features huge, mature trees that dripped with rain that morning. The plaque embedded in concrete reads: "Award-winning poet, scholar, professor at Victoria College, activist, and devoted friend, Jay was a long-time local resident. A modest person of great wit, she was a spirited champion of liveable and inclusive cities that respect heritage, public space, and parks. Jay Macpherson enriched our world." I think of Macpherson with her epic vision of anagogic man, history's rebellious daughters and the traditions of late Romance, and think she'd like the rain's biblical connotations.

I head east to Yonge and then south to find a marker for the Indigenous portage, Gete-Onigaming or the Carrying-Place Trail, at Davenport Road. The trail was a path along the shore between the Don and Humber Rivers when Lake Ontario's shore was right where Davenport is now. Legend has it that William Lyon Mackenzie burned down a house at this corner during the Upper Canada Rebellion in 1837, but I am tired just thinking of that colonial history, which seemed like nothing to be proud of when I first moved to Toronto as a young woman and is even less so now. The city tears itself down and rebuilds itself constantly, sometimes in ways that make it unrecognizable. I think of the woman in Leeds who demanded to know if I was thinking of buying the house I appeared to be staring at, and the look on her face when I pointed to the wood pigeon I was watching – incredulous, like I was a bit of an idiot. The words on the Gete-Onigaming sign look back at me, footsore and damp, wet hair plastered to my head, idiotic in my own way. I turn and go back to the hotel, where the doorman looks a little reluctant at the sight of the drowned ghost in front of him but sweeps the door open nonetheless so I can squelch through the lobby.

*

Long after that walk, I discovered that Jay Macpherson had actually lived south of the green on tiny Berryman Street – John Berryman, more poet connections! She was a private person, and I know she'd hate the fact that I found her address through a real estate blog that displayed photos of her house as it was sold after her death. The blog attracted potential buyers by noting that an award-winning writer had once owned the house and showing photos of the rooms in which she had lived and wrote for decades. I stared at her office with reverent curiosity. The original house was built in 1888 and was advertised as having all its original features. The next owners gutted it, renovated it and flipped it. It sold for three million dollars, and the real estate blog gleefully updated their original post with photos of the house's new look. I wonder if the current owners have read *The Boatman*, the book for which Macpherson won a Governor General's Award, and if they know that they live where she honed her "third eye [that] saw through order like a glass / To concentrate, refine and rarify." Probably not.

When it is raining – and isn't it always? – the farther you are from a person or object, the more their image is obscured. Some scientists say mammals are evolutionarily advantaged to see through rain, and others dispute that we can see through it at all, citing Olbers' paradox, which proposes that our inability to see well in obscured conditions pushes back against our ideas of space as infinite. In other words, seeing poorly through rain is not a factor of photon travel or the velocity of droplet strikes but poor visibility telling us hard truths about space – that it is not infinite. When we slow down enough to look, to see our pasts melt away via gentrification, to dream of the public monuments we'd like to see, questions of infinity and perfect visibility become moot.

I was walking with my partner by the Grand River when a woman came along the path toward us, an off-leash golden retriever by her side. My partner can be a stickler about leash laws so he took himself off to the side, and moved ahead. I watched the dog, who never seemed to stray far from the woman's side, and thought the lack of leash didn't bear mentioning. I greeted her as she came closer. She said, "It's so beautiful, isn't it?," gesturing to the river and the trees close by, the mallards and geese riding the current. We stopped to talk for a minute, and she told me that she had inherited the family home after being away for many years, and she was just starting to get to know the place again – the city, the trails, its culture and wild spaces. Partway through the conversation, I realized that she had transitioned. It's hard to be trans anywhere, especially in smaller cities. I listened as she talked about exploring the same trails now that she had when she was a kid. It was clear that this was a place of refuge and rediscovery of all kinds. I reminded her of what was ahead on the trail – a plaque marking a traditional Haudenosaunee hunting ground, and a rock outcropping that would give her a spectacular view of the river – and we said goodbye. When I caught up with my partner, he asked, "What did she say?" I told him the truth: we talked about being women walking in the woods.

Crawford Lake

The forest knew things had gotten out of hand. It all started with some trees who believed they were carvings: butterflies or wolves or giant hands reaching up from the ground holding bulbous sparrows. These trees thought the other trees jealous, seeing them strut into elegant but alien shapes. And were the carvings covetous of the trees' height, the way they were always budding, then leafing, then dropping leaves to stand naked against the clouds? The meromictic lake was deeper than it was wide, and it was smarter than it was kind. The lake allowed, at his coldest level, that he was misunderstood. He was more Clark Gable than Spencer Tracy – never one for mixing. He resented the way the boardwalk circled him, the way her boards creaked like she knew his refusal to mingle and judged him for it. But the boardwalk wasn't even thinking of the lake; she had her own problems.

A Card-Carrying Member of the Bad Birders' Club

identifies a blue jay carrying a peanut in its beak as a new species, gets excited about juncos like tiny two-tone court shoes, lets the squirrels shred the suet in the feeder, wants a necklace made of tree swallows (jk: not really; a little), stops to watch crows swoop because they might be but never are hawks, defaults to red-tailed for every hawk, hasn't seen an owl in two seasons, has three times earned rogue status on birding sites, puts up the purple martin house too early and now can't get the sparrows out, is dive-bombed by chickadees and chased by geese, posts blurred photos of brownish or whitish objects. Call 1-800-BAD-BIRD now to stumble around and squint, to say to each other *wait what's that where over there that's amazing whaaaaat*

The Trouble with FaunaWatch

I went into the woods because I wanted to live deliberately, to front
only the essential facts of life, and see if I could not learn what it
had to teach, and not, when I came to die, discover that I had not
lived.

– Henry David Thoreau, *Walden*

PROPOSITION: INTO THE WOODS

I went into the woods near my house because I thought I could learn.
I was deliberate, but the task was not that simple. Absolutely nothing about observing animals, or writing about observing animals,
is simple, the way that nothing about being the owner-operator of a
fleshy human body is simple.

PRACTICE: WATCHING

When Congress 2011 was held at the university where I teach, I
hosted two other scholars at my home. We were in the living room
talking over the day's cache of papers and keynotes when the cat
stiffened to attention in the front window. We looked out to see a
raccoon on the lawn. Raccoons are notoriously fastidious about
their food, often washing it – and their paws – before eating, but this

raccoon could not have been less choosy. She ripped up the grass, snapped up one end of an earthworm, and yanked it centimetre by centimetre from the ground with her jaws, stretching it taut as an elastic band. When the worm finally snapped out of the ground and the raccoon crammed the length of it – still wriggling – into her mouth, we shouted in triumph. It was brutal; it was ravenous; it was the most fascinating display we had seen all day. Did we exoticize the sight? Did we think of this as a problem? If we did, no one mentioned it.

For a few years, I posted my daily fauna sightings on Facebook, a series of updates that I called FaunaWatch. I made the format intentionally spare: the designation or hashtag *FaunaWatch*, a location and a list of non-human beings seen that day in my (mostly) urban life. A typical day's post may have read, "FaunaWatch Waterloo to Kitchener: five wild turkeys by Highway 8, red-tailed hawk above Conestoga, rabbit on median at Bridgeport." Farther afield, the post could read, "FaunaWatch San Francisco: brown pelican in harbour, twenty goats on Russian Hill, flock of green-and-peach parrots near Coit Tower." But most are duller: "FaunaWatch backyard: cardinal, downy woodpecker, and juncos at feeder. Neighbourhood chipmunk." The practice was always the same: see, post, repeat. It recalled the life lists or yearly lists kept by dedicated birders, though with two important distinctions. The FaunaWatch posts included mammals, insects and reptiles, as well as birds; and repetition was important, especially to the local postings. I might have seen the same rabbit three days in a row, or I might have been unable to distinguish between the flock of wild turkeys in one part of the Laurel Creek Conservation Area and what appeared to be but was not necessarily a different flock in another part of the conservation area on two separate occasions. That ravenous raccoon on the lawn appeared as a FaunaWatch posting.

For a while, the practice of listing fooled me into thinking of

FaunaWatch as a dip into the pool where the everyday mixes with the notable. The postings slipped easily into the banal, particularly when contrasted with the excitements of urban culture often featured in the status updates of others: hilarious or crazy-making online articles, births, deaths, exasperated declarations of odd encounters. Yet, as a practice, the FaunaWatch project multiplied in complexity precisely because it had humble (and humbling) beginnings, growing as it did out of my intense desire to fix myself in the realities of my new geographical location in southwestern Ontario.

I moved to the area because of my university appointment; though I had lived in Toronto before, I am originally from the Prairies and knew nothing about Ontario life outside the GTA. Like many small Canadian cities, Waterloo has material advantages in its clean air, green urban space and surrounding farmland, and some cultural challenges including a literary scene that depends on a few stalwart citizens and a main drag that caters to student drinking culture. My sense of displacement grew when I bought a house and became fully immersed in the anxiety brought on by my commitment to a small plot of land and the building atop it. A lifelong habit of hyperbole propelled me into the stratosphere at the mere mention of a broken window or a purchase larger than a vacuum cleaner.

Until I heard chirping coming from the basement.

My first apocalyptic thought was that the basement had a plague of frogs, but I listened some more; it was a cricket singing in the cool damp of the cellar. I remembered Dickens's *The Cricket on the Hearth* and George Selden's *The Cricket in Times Square*, neither of which I had read in many years; both authors suggested that the cricket was a good-luck charm for a household. That cricket sang for several weeks in the basement; I never found him, but he stuck in my mind. The next spring, I found a live muskrat trapped under our chain-link fence. She was wedged under the angle of the link, and it was clear that unless she got free, one of the neighbourhood cats could make short work of her. I had a strange moment, though, when I first spotted her. Not only could I not remember the name for the creature, I found her unrecognizable despite having seen many muskrats along the Seine and La Salle Rivers in Manitoba. My seconds of misrecognition were both disconcerting and freeing; it was, frankly, a relief to look and not know anything. Jacques Derrida calls this experience the moment of "following," when the watcher is caught in a gaze that philosophically strips them naked, and compares the moment to being caught in the sight of "a seer" or "visionary." The moment could not last. I went inside and told my partner we had an animal trapped under the fence. He came out with some wire cutters and clipped the link that trapped her, and she slipped free and ran away. I took a photo as she ran, in which she appears as a fuzzy shape among a tangle of garden tools in our neighbours' driveway – unrecognizable once again. But that muskrat made me curious. I could not figure out how she had made it so far from the river. But a map showed that Laurel Creek ran through our neighbourhood, just a block and a half away.

We moved close by the Laurel Creek Conservation Area in 2010, and I joined Facebook shortly after. When two wild turkeys landed on our driveway in November of that year, I had to mention it on Facebook as a bizarre neighbourhood occurrence. I noted, too, the merlin that we spotted in the backyard and the geese that passed so low overhead that I could hear them breathing. In doing so, I felt the return of an old practice, born of all the long camping trips of my childhood.

In a classic example of future writers who write their first "books" in spiral-bound notebooks, as a kid I had kept what I called a camp diary that noted the day's animal sightings, often illustrated and filled with useful information about how to recognize each animal by appearance, habitat and characteristics. These descriptions grew more elaborate over time, as other children that I met would call chipmunks squirrels, or frogs toads, or deer moose, and my kid-self grew infuriated by their casual grasp of what seemed to me to be so specific. My brother and I spent four to six weeks a year as unplugged as it got – no television, only a handful of books and the car radio (controlled by my father and only when we drove from one site to another). This was before the days of hot showers or electrical hookups at campsites. The more rustic the campsite, the higher my father valued it as a destination. Some places could not really be called campsites by today's standards; they were just spots by a lake with road access. We saw a lot of deer and a lot of bears, and because this was long before the wildlife had become used to the presence of humans, most times the animals looked us over and headed in the other direction – we were neither familiar nor strange, they just didn't want any part of us. We were taught that wild animals were different from our pets, and that while they were fascinating, they had a right to space and respect. We were visitors in their neighbourhood.

Perversely, nothing made me feel more like a visitor to a neighbourhood than owning a home, so I wanted to watch and learn from the area's previous inhabitants, including the animals and birds that lived there. So FaunaWatch grew by chance and by design. I pulled the title from Alissa York's *Fauna*, a novel about the confluence of animal and human life living in the Don Valley, and added the tongue-in-cheek suffix *Watch* to connote urgency (NewsWatch! StormWatch!) and humour. I had been using the title for more than a year when I learned about an Australian wildlife preservation society and a non-profit organization based in the Netherlands using the same name – people across the world from each other, thinking similar thoughts. But while both of the other groups have websites and memberships, my FaunaWatch practice was just me and a loose collection of friends who chimed in with pictures and sightings. FaunaWatch also opened up to me the lives of people I know who are avid citizen scientists and amateur naturalists, as my father had been: birders, volunteer conservation wardens, backyard chicken keepers. People who are aware of the necessity, and the ironies, of negotiating space alongside animals.

Because the plan from the beginning was to look carefully to see with whom I was sharing space, I made some discoveries about how the wild and the urban interact in my bioregion. May to June is groundhog season, and not a week passes during that time when I don't see at least one with the incredible insouciant quality of a large rodent with all the time in the world. Wild turkeys live and breed in family units of about four adults and seven to nine chicks in the conservation area, with June to September as prime spotting season. Herons frequent the Columbia reservoir as well as the reservoir at Laurel Creek, but orioles prefer the forest canopy at the Columbia reservoir. In the winter, small mammals beat a path through the snow beside our fence, which we called the "Little Paw Highway" – we saw plenty of rabbit, squirrel, chipmunk and raccoon footprints. But our elderly neighbour told us to watch for a mammal that liked garbage; he described it as a grey rat but much, much bigger. He could not think of the name of the creature, and I too had a few minutes of blankness. What was this animal that could not be named? We eventually saw opossum pawprints, which looked disconcertingly like the handprints of a human baby, lost in the snow.

I can't fool myself into thinking that I am a good citizen scientist. The cornfields two blocks from my house are apparently full of horned larks, according to a local birding website, yet I have never seen one. Time, season, location and happenstance rule the day. My unwritten FaunaWatch rule was that there is strength in happenstance and being in a certain place at an unplanned time can provide the best of opportunities. Expect the unexpected.

PROBLEMS: IMPLICATED WATCHING

> Wildness requires no organizational intervention, even of the purest and most democratic sort. Wildness is whole. It is the antithesis of the domesticated human state, uncontaminated by power, claims to power, or the need for power.
> – John A. Livingston, *Rogue Primate*

At the beginning, FaunaWatch needed some parameters regarding how to look and how to write who or what I saw. I developed some rules that seemed sensible enough to follow and challenging enough to keep my attention. But these rules swiftly revealed themselves to be full of holes and constantly in need of adjustment. I list them here in all their fallibility:

- Notice and record simply.
- Identify; do not editorialize.
- State; do not make poetic.
- Photo evidence is not necessary; be willing to be thought a liar.
- Resist urges to exoticize, to fictionalize or to narrate.
- Wield the gaze and accept the blame.
- Consider who "counts."

If nature abhors a vacuum, then it also despises human rules. Livingston's admonition that "wildness is whole" and utterly beyond the human need for organization reminds me that these rules were for me, not for nature. I turned to taxonomy, but it was perplexing, especially when it seemed the most certain. Were insects fauna as I construed it? Were reptiles? Were people? What was the place of domestic animals in FaunaWatch? Of livestock? Who "counts" as significant or worthy of mention changes with the seasons, with the locale, with the weather. If the idea was to produce an accurate record, then I should list every sparrow, every robin, every grey squirrel, every ubiquitous chickadee. I changed the rule to "list common fauna when they do something different or unusual." That turned out to be even worse, for what is "different"? The impact of urban environments on fauna suggests that the animals must constantly adapt to the presence of more trees, fewer trees, different kinds of trees, less bush, more feeders, new houses, more traffic. The amount of construction within a ten-block radius of my house on the rural edge of a small city was considerable: the construction of four major low-rise office buildings with accompanying parking lots, service roads, road widening and traffic signals; and an ever-expanding housing development a few blocks to the west. What was "unusual" behaviour under these constantly changing conditions? Canada geese and mallards swamped the construction sites each spring, swimming in the puddles and water-filled ditches made by earth-movers. Some species' responses to climate change meant that my bird identification book was outdated almost right away – it noted that bald eagles were "rare to locally uncommon" in my bioregion, but as the winters became warmer, I would see five or six of these eagles per year, confirmed by sightings posted on local birder websites. So much for the timeless habits of birds and animals.

My rules about how to post were also tested. Friends laughed when I told them that I would resist making FaunaWatch posts poetic. How do you write *fox* or *goldfinch* and not trigger a bucolic response? I discovered a whole different problem with negotiating appeal, as well. I had "Guest FaunaWatches" in which I posted a wildlife video that underscored the mix of human and animal interaction, but I resisted posting cute things domestic animals had been trained to do. How to then deal with the sight of a tabby hunting in the conservation area? I chose to include it in a FaunaWatch post on the basis that it was performing wildness, but that lead to a reader suggestion that I, too, am performing wildness, as were the students frequenting the downtown bars, the participants in the local Pride parade and everyone who attended Oktoberfest.

When is a list not a list? What about the problem of character? Seeing picturesque and hopeful rabbits in the early spring, it's easy to think of them as the smart and serious protagonists of *Watership Down*; come summer, they turn into thieving vermin eating from gardens. And what about my own "character"? I had to note how I was using the animals – as psychological ballast, as writing material, as (sometimes) false evidence of rootedness. If a camera lens eroticizes the object that it reproduces, as Roland Barthes suggests, what is the lens of the human eye doing to the observed animal? When I made a list, this was undoubtedly part of mourning the animals, for to seek them out as unusual or abundant examples of bioregionality was to note at the same time their vulnerability.

What is an exchange of looks between beings? What is appropriation? My intention to keep things humble exacerbated the complexities and tensions of looking. Noting the existence of other beings has a smack of saviour complex about it, as though my attention gives the other being a life they would not have had otherwise. The project reminded me that thinking about rootedness or present-ness, like almost everything else that is important, may be absolutely necessary, but it can also be dangerously naive. My sense of irony was jump-started as well, for every opportunity that made FaunaWatch possible was also that which made it impossible, and vice versa. For example, I spent twenty minutes in the backyard with one of the rabbits brave enough (or hungry enough) not to flee, and as I spoke quietly to her, admiring the unusual red fur on her legs, what I imagined to be our communion was undercut by the fact that my enormous, marauding species takes up space that she (and the generations of rabbits before her) used to occupy. The biggest irony may be that often my view of nature takes place from the window provided for me by a fossil fuel–burning vehicle, often on the way to boarding an even bigger fossil fuel–burning vehicle. But there are surprises, too. The major highways that cut through natural spaces become raptor corridors, as hawks and eagles take advantage of the shorter, well-maintained grass beside the pavement to hunt and turkey vultures take advantage of the frequent roadkill. This was good for FaunaWatch, but I'm not sure that we should all be singing "Circle of Life" at this discovery. History is full of stories of species overbalance that eventually rights itself, but in the shifting sands of climate change, I wonder about the abilities of such overbalance to right itself quickly, easily or at all.

When I began the FaunaWatch project, I did not expect my specialty in elegiac work to have any bearing on how I wrote, but the borders of liveness and deadness are unavoidable when thinking about animals. A scholar who had just delivered a paper on Yann Martel's *Life of Pi* sneered distastefully when I asked what he thought about Martel's more controversial novel, *Beatrice and Virgil*. "I prefer my animals alive," he sniffed. So do I, but dead animals are so much a part of North American life that they cannot be dismissed as mere grotesquerie or recipients of human cruelty, though they may be those as well. Alissa York and I were on our way back from seeing deer in RIM Park when we fell to discussing roadkill's position in FaunaWatch. I had been reluctant to list the animals I saw by the side of the road – so many raccoons and squirrels and rabbits and cats – but the sightings were often significant: a coyote's body feathering away to nothing on the gravel shoulder of a local road; the first opossum I ever saw on an on-ramp to the 401; the still porcupine by the Trans-Canada, just outside of Regina; the hindquarters of a deer I saw in a ditch on the way up to Ontario cottage country. Alissa made the smart observation that dead animals appear prominently in two of her novels – as taxidermy subjects in *Effigy* and as roadkill in *Fauna* – because dead animals remain still under a prolonged gaze. You can get a good long look – something that writers and artists need. In addition, I read and admired David Adams Richards's memoir *Facing the Hunter: Reflections on a Misunderstood Way of*

Life, not because I always agreed with him but because he wrote convincingly about the role that class plays in people's relationship to animals, arguing that most hunters are conservationists. He made me rethink the relationship that many people in Canada have with animals as a food source to be treated with respect. FaunaWatch thereafter included the quick and the dead.

The ultimate FaunaWatch irony may be about the priority granted to looking. It is hard not to look up at a cardinal flying by when someone is talking. It is also rude to watch a cardinal in flight when you are listening to someone talk. Posturing and preening can be a common practice among citizen scientists and nature writers, and while I think myself diligent about rooting this out of my posts, I can't say how successful I am – or am not – at this. Seeing animals can be a reminder to be humble, whatever that means in a capitalist society where even memories can have undertones of material acquisition. A record is a notation; like an elegy, it acts against forgetting, but a record neither revives life nor defies entropy.

POLITICS: FIRST PERSON, MULTIPLE ANIMALS

I rarely post in FaunaWatch anymore, but the practice – with its shifting rules and hungry gaze – made me think differently about the lyric mode, and the place of living beings as tropes or even as rungs on the lyric ladder. Beautiful though they are, and as much as I admire the sight of them, birds do not make my heart soar with poetry; they don't justify my ragged existence. But it's better to look than not, better to see than ignore. Or is it? The strangely alienating dynamics of FaunaWatch made my writing more vulnerable to a stutter, more given to questions of the manipulation of imagery. I feel hyperaware of what Dana Medoro and Alison Calder have called "the volatility of the human-animal relationship." Calder's poem "We Hate the Animals," with its reminders of "scabrous sparrows, shitting pigeons, / raccoons who strew our garbage on the lawn," is a testament to the urbanite's complex and deeply ironic relationship with nature as both transcendent in isolation and repulsive in interaction:

> In darkness animals knock cans, chew bags,
> spread trash as if we meant it to be seen.
> They eat our trash, they are our trash,
> they must be taken out and lost, like trash.
> Oh how we hate the animals,
> hate what we think we've made.

Calder's final line points to the control we exert over animal image when we cannot control animal behaviour, including the ability to take them out and lose them if we want. The *I* in the act of observation offers the most enduring question about the politics of looking: If the animals multiply and move, and even move close to the watcher, the observation becomes increasingly autobiographical. If I see a bald eagle on the ice of the reservoir in February, the eagle is the important – and most amazing! – being, but my watching tells the story. I began the FaunaWatch project as a way to take my attention off myself, but my autobiographical impulse grew the more I invested in this labour of love, in pursuit of what I could no longer ignore. In his essay "Unpacking My Library: A Talk about Book Collecting," Walter Benjamin asked: "For what else is this collection but a disorder to which habit has accommodated itself to such an extent that it can appear as order?" There's no denying that FaunaWatch became a habit, and that habit became practice. I know that this practice "appears as order," especially in written form. In FaunaWatch, the order of reporting and listing were collector's tools, accommodated to the chaos of chance, effort and desire. I hadn't wanted to leave the house on the day of the bald eagle sighting; it was cold and blustery, with the snow arcing off the open fields in great gusts in front of my car. The driver in the car behind me kept revving his engine and riding my bumper, and I pulled over to let him by. And that's when I saw the eagle. He was large, and wet, and marching up and down the length of a small opening in the creek ice, pausing to sip water every minute or so. No other life was evident: no geese, no songbirds; only the occasional car driving by. It was just the eagle and me for a while. He set his raptor's eyes on me, the only object with a heat signature in the February landscape. Then he shrugged his wings like Ed Asner in an episode of *Lou Grant* and lifted off. And then he was like nothing else but an eagle.

Benjamin again: "Every passion borders on the chaotic, but the collector's passion borders on the chaos of memories." Life is so short, and our creatureliness so apparent as we grow older, that all we can do is let our collections teach us the pleasure of chaos.

Birdwatching for Beginners

An Incomplete Quiz

1. If two great egrets appear in a pond by a highway in northern Ontario in June and the observer is in the passenger seat of a car driving at 120 km/hour, how quickly will expert birders tell her she didn't see the egrets?
   a) within twenty minutes of posting on Facebook
   b) within two minutes on iNaturalist
   c) pics or it didn't happen
   d) how is this a question

2. The best way to distinguish between a soaring hawk and an ambitious crow is:
   a) flight pattern
   b) plumage
   c) size
   d) bird poems are so 1988

3. When you spot two rabbits in the morning, do you interpret this as a sign for:
- a) warm weather
- b) fecundity
- c) clear and present danger
- d) the inability of the quiz compiler to focus on birds

4. When your elderly neighbour welcomes you to the neighbour-hood and says, "Be careful of the . . ." and then can't remember the name of the animal he describes, do you:
- a) assume he means a raccoon
- b) prepare for the animal apocalypse
- c) become immediately distracted by a loathsome fantasy in which you lift the garbage can lid to find a hissing and possibly fainting opossum
- d) become immediately distracted by a lovely fantasy in which you lift the garbage can lid to find a hissing and possibly fainting opossum

5. Your photographer friend sees a heron standing in a pond and wants a photo of the bird with its wings spread. He asks you to toss a stick to startle the heron. Do you:
- a) choose a stick carefully and aim to miss
- b) tell him to toss his own damn stick
- c) throw a stick at the photographer to see if he startles
- d) slowly raise one leg and stretch your neck forward

6. When you see a falcon's nest atop a light standard viewable from your mother's hospital room, do you:
   a) get her into a wheelchair and take her to the window to look
   b) believe her when she says she can see the nest from the bed
   c) sit in the hospital's Miracle Garden on the tenth of the sixteen days of her dying and listen to the young falcons peeping in their high voices
   d) why are you even thinking of birds – you are the worst

7. When you spot a three-legged dog at any time during your day, do you:
   a) interpret it as a sign that you'll see two rabbits the next morning
   b) reject the sight as inspo-porn
   c) pursue it for a selfie
   d) remember a joke about a three-legged dog named Tripod and wonder if that was the whole joke or if there was more to it

8. When you say that you are writing poems about how disconnected you feel from the natural world, and how there were years so bad you thought you would die and the only thing that saved you each day was a walk by the creek, and the other writer snorts and says, "That's a cliché," do you:
   a) say nothing
   b) say, "Saying *that's a cliché* is a cliché!"
   c) listen to a tinny version of your own voice in your head yelling, "Walk away!"
   d) walk away

9. When next you see a bird, you think:
   a) there's a bird
   b) there's a poem
   c) there
   d) *

Take Daily

Patient: Author, scholar, occasional madwoman
Medication: Quotidian pedestrianism
Common uses: Temporarily relieves symptoms of overt humanity, extremities of affect, mental spiralling, inferno awareness, over-thinking, hyperventilation
Frequency: As often as you can stand it

*

A long, low moan quavered through the open front window, accompanied by a middle-aged man with a cane who paused every couple of steps. I admired his vocalization, a song of frustration and effort, determination and breath. He walked like someone recovering from surgery whose physiotherapist had assigned him a daily walk twice around the block. The moan was functional; it was part of how he made it around the block. I didn't lean out of the window and ask if he was all right, because he was and was not all right. He was in the pain that comes with any body: injury, disease, aging, surgeries. This pain was not to be borne silently, and as much as I wanted to yell, "Solidarity, brother!" I thought this would be presumptuous. Now I think I should have done it anyway. There's very little language for applauding the public performance of pain that doesn't lean on judgment or diagnosis.

In *The Waves*, Virginia Woolf wrote that pain for which words are lacking should "be held in solitude," and that part of the confusion of pain is that the sounds that issue from it appear simultaneously "very remote and then very close." So I kept my ears open as he made his rounds and listened for that intimate moaning, made public twice daily. After two weeks, the moaning stopped. Now, I see him most days when I walk the neighbourhood and we exchange waves and nods. He's recovered now, a little hesitant on his feet, a little older, as I am, too. I wave because his consistently negotiated relationship to walking makes him one of my people.

*

You know the story. March 2020: a last in-person class or meeting, news trickling in about other universities and colleges shutting their doors, and then it's you and your institution, your colleagues, your students. Then the scramble of the following weekend: writing instructions for students, trying to anticipate their questions, moving all teaching materials online. As for me, I rewrote and adapted an eighty-minute interactive lesson into a thirty-minute recorded lecture and online discussion; with my inexperience with the technology, the planning for a single remote class took a whole day. My birthday disappeared, unnoticed and uncelebrated. It didn't occur to me that I could have cancelled classes, more fool me. I prepped and taught online using technology I hadn't heard of six days previously, and answered many anxious emails. Whenever I stood up from my desk, my back snapped at me like unfed alligators in the world's most obscure reptile park. My students and I finished the teaching term. Some of them wrote to thank me for taking such good care of them. I only wish I had taken better care of myself.

I have degenerative disc disease and a shrieking sciatic nerve. When advised by my doctor that for day-to-day pain control I was to stand up every twenty minutes, my first thought was not for my aching bod; it was instead about how standing up so frequently would interrupt my workflow. But chronic pain seems like exaggeration or impossibility, even when you are in it. I catch myself thinking, "Again?," as pain shoots down my leg, as though I haven't lived for more than a decade with it, as though ease of movement is my right. My chronic pain ebbs and flows; it allows some activities one day and not the next; it circumscribes my choices and forces me to consider mundane details that contribute to – or decrease – my mobility on any given day. I'm forced to consider what I'm wearing, where I'm sitting and for how long, what I'm carrying, how I'm bending or standing. I believe in good days and bad days; I believe in the alleviation of pain, for an hour, a day, a week, but being a professor – the long hours spent in front of a screen or bent over books and papers, the constant needs assessment, my machine-like habit of forgetting that I need rest – has never been kind to my body.

When I leave my massage appointment, my RMT says, "Drink lots of water and go for a short walk if you can." I walk the paved trail of a creekside park, striving to keep the benefits of deep massage. My legs feel like they are the same length for the first time in weeks and the ping of my glutes is a good ache and not tearing pain. My feet are firm and flexible on the ground. But the moment I see other people, I shift slightly away from my newly perfected balance, tipping back into old bodily habits. And this signals that the after-treatment walk is over – it's time to go home and drink lots of water. Italo Calvino, in his amazing book *Invisible Cities*, reminds us: "Seek and learn to recognize who and what, in the midst of inferno, are not inferno, then make them endure, give them space." The ability to identify who is not inferno is a consummate human skill. In other words, hell is other people, except when it's not.

*

Directions: Open door and leave house. Walk away from house for fifteen minutes. Breathe. Keep your eyes open. Walk back to house for fifteen minutes. Go back in house.

Some days, you may look at the sky, either from the backyard or from the side of the house where no one else goes. Your neighbours' tall fence and the raspberry canes will hide you.

Patient Allergies: Simple solutions to complex problems.

*

I often mistype *grade* as *garde* – good evidence of semantic slippage. To grade is to guard: standards, the institution, evaluative methods that may be outmoded. We stand on grade for thee.

April 2020 began with relief from anxiety prep and technology risks, but there was suddenly a new and intense form of online coaching to get my students through finals month. Papers came in and I dove into grading, and then received multiple emails about how, when and why to grade from the administration, many of whom had neither taught nor graded before. Finally, after the traditional three-week grading period had stretched to seven, I graded my final student paper, posted the grades and did not feel relief. Instead, I felt dread move in me like a tapeworm.

Like one out of five women in Canada, I'm a sexual assault survivor. And like many women, I am adept at burying myself in work. But as soon as I was untethered from support tasks in spring 2020, I started to have nearly day-length panic attacks. For weeks in May, they rolled over me in waves that yanked me from sleep at 3:00 a.m., weakening around noon and abating in mid-afternoon. I would arrive at 2:00 p.m. sweating as though I had run ten kilometres but grateful to be back, even for a few hours, to "normal." Panic attacks weren't a new part of my life, but before this, they had always been relatively short-lived: a bad two hours plus a jittery day. But I ignored the lay of the land; I had completely glossed over the rough autumn of 2019 when I repeatedly twisted myself into knots over situations I could not control. In other words, I was already depleted.

A few days turned into a week, and I couldn't get my doctor on the phone. Left to my own devices and with global pandemic case numbers growing, I tried a lot of things: increased vitamin B, CBD oil, quitting caffeine cold turkey. I stopped listening to the news. I dropped off social media. I rode a stationary bike for hours. I withdrew two articles that were scheduled for publication because I couldn't recognize the person who had written them. I couldn't concentrate long enough to read because the inside of my head was a fiery loop. If the hospitals hadn't been full of COVID patients, I would have admitted myself.

I called a drop-in clinic and was told by the doctor on call that he couldn't prescribe anything to me because I might be an addict. (And you, *sir*, might not be a doctor, and yet we're both going to have to trust each other.) He asked if I was in danger of killing myself. I said, "Just the opposite; I think someone is coming to kill me." He said okay and hung up.

Okay?

*

How to use this medicine: Take once daily. Pay no attention to the step counters behind the curtain. Raise one foot, lean forward, catch yourself. Raise the other, lean forward. Repeat.

Take this medication for a full course of treatment. Do not skip days because you are bored or too cold or too hot or crying too much. Do not skip because everything is the same. Do not skip because you are the same. Do not skip because you'll never be the same.

Active ingredients: Vitamin D; hope sweat; obedience.

Before Using this Medicine: *^?

*

If you've never had a panic attack, I'll say first that I wouldn't wish the experience on anyone. The experience for me has always been at once feeling hyper-present and adrift, floundering in quicksand, kicking and not finding the bottom of the pit. Because my body is convinced that I am dying, it flushes blood to where it seems to be needed the most: the brain. Or, more specifically, the primal or reptile brain. My Anxiety Kraken awakens, unfurls its tentacles and then I have a fight (or flight) on my hands.

I've just described a panic attack with imagery drawn from Warner Bros. cartoons and old episodes of *Sea Hunt*. Trauma descriptions often default to images consumed at the time of trauma – in my case, early adolescence. Panic attacks are awful because while they fixate on a material circumstance, they defy the logic of that circumstance. Statements that the sky is not falling are not reassuring to people who have had the sky crack open their skulls. Body logic is immensely strong.

To enumerate the entangled causes of my panic attacks would be to suggest that they are explainable, or that they obey an accessible logic. At the start of pandemic restrictions, I was admittedly a little smug, because suddenly everyone was going to experience what traumatized people all over the world have experienced: restricted freedoms, the need to keep a distance, the feeling of being a little trapped all the time, the understanding that what others think is invisible or don't believe in could kill you. But living under official restrictions that mirrored in so many ways my unofficial life, I slipped and then was in deep and sputtering for breath. I was afraid to go outside and afraid to stay in. When I was outside, I felt the sky reaching into my brain. When I was inside, I felt the walls pressing in on me. There was nowhere to go. Fresh out of strategies, I sat in the passenger seat while my partner drove me around the country roads north of where we lived. Sometimes the distraction of passing open fields and farmhouses helped, sometimes it didn't.

On one of those long country drives, I couldn't feel my legs. I slapped and pinched my thighs; I could feel a bit of sensation, so they weren't totally numb, but they didn't feel like the supporting columns of my torso. My legs were like Slinkies, weirdly uncontrollable. They felt unstable even though I was sitting down, and I wondered how I'd get out of the car. Would my legs slip out from under me and dump me onto the ground? Maybe I would careen upwards like an untethered Macy's parade balloon, out of control and headed for the stratosphere. When I told John, he looked over at me and said something brilliant: "Would you like to have a bit of a yell?"

My decision-making skills were at an all-time low, but I sat up straight because I knew how to do this. We looked for an open field on a minor road, one without nearby houses or barns. I got out, John made sure I could stand, and then I staggered twenty metres up the road to get a little space from the car. It was about 7:30 a.m., and the lonely road was all browns and greys under cloud cover; on my right was a field backed by a long windbreak of conifers. As I wobbled on my wet-spaghetti legs, I started to stomp my boots into the gravel as hard as I could. I put all my weight into it, trying to dent the gravel with big footprints. And it worked a little, I could feel the muscles in my thighs start to tingle. I stopped and faced the field; lifted my right knee as high as it would go and slammed down my foot. The jolt rode up my body and rattled my torso. I looked back at John, who sat in the driver's seat and discreetly pretended to watch something across the road while keeping one eye on me. I kept stomping, trying to move the sensation into my calves. With every thud I shouted a syllable. I had done such things years before in acting workshops; however, it is one thing to shout at your scene partner in a timed exercise and another to stand on the edge of a field alone and shout, "*I. Can't. Feel. My legs.*"

I shouted a lot more. The phrase I kept returning to is a gold standard among assault survivors: "It's my body." And was it ever. It was my body, in all its pain and numbness; it was my body driving my brain crazy and vice versa. I shouted it over and over on that roadside, aiming my voice at the trees. I heard the mashing of my boots as they displaced tiny stones. If I heard a car coming, I feigned a casual stroll until the vehicle passed, then I started stomping again. No one pulled over. No one even slowed down. No one wants to know about a woman yelling by the side of the road.

It ended with a bird. I was taking in breath to shout when a small hawk swooped over the field. I laughed and shouted at once, a spontaneous sound that told me I had made it back to a working body. There was no point in scaring away all the mice – that hawk had to eat. I walked back to the car.

Later that day, I found a name online for what afflicted me. "Jelly legs" are common symptoms in panic attacks when the blood is shunted elsewhere in the body to find and defeat the threat. The treatment is, no surprise, exercise, even though stomping and yelling into a field was not mentioned. However, I recommend it.

The relief was temporary, but it was still an important discovery. Getting my body back on a more permanent basis was going to take effort, noise and a willingness to perform some social effrontery. Yelling into a field was going to be the least of it. I was going to have to rest; I was going to have to say no to opportunities. I was going to have to figure out how to be the scholar I was rather than the scholar that the patriarchy wanted me to be: the always-available but always-inadequate mother. In case of emotional labour, break glass.

*

Do not use this treatment: If you are currently experiencing spiking professional paranoia. In case of, contact your physician, herbalist, therapist, sisters, partner and best friends. You need all hands on deck.

Additional possible side effects: Ability to identify birdsong. Ability to nickname neighbourhood kids. Expanding definitions of public art. Burrs. Scratches. Blisters.

*

My doctor was unavailable for two weeks. This was in the early weeks of pandemic restrictions, and doctors had their hands full. But when I finally heard from her, she prescribed for me – along with an SSRI – a daily walk, speaking as though anti-anxiety drugs were a good idea but the walk was essential. She stressed that the walk did not need to be especially athletic or goal-focused, beyond leaving the house under my own power. Some people have been checking which routes through their neighbourhoods will earn them ten thousand steps a day, but my mental health was precarious and my standards were blessedly low.

A friend introduced me to cemetery walks, which had a lot of advantages during pandemic restrictions. The avenues were wide, good for social distancing and to see others approaching, and almost always plowed in the winter. Walking by thousands of graves weekly doesn't automatically do the work of memento mori, but I found it remarkably settling to recall, in desperate times, that death is not a terrifying news item or a breaking headline but something personal, memorialized, tended to. Not everyone is lucky enough to have such a beautiful resting place, or even to have such a spot to walk, but there was something about passing by all those quiet headstones that calmed me.

Like taking medication at the same time every day, walking the same route every day suggests calm, routine, maintenance. It allows me to notice changes, small and large, in both the neighbourhood and myself. I venture into green spaces like stormwater ponds, creek banks, woodlots and cemeteries. In these spaces where human presence is allowed though not encouraged, I take my reptile brain walking with a leash around its scaly neck. It goes almost willingly now, and sniffs at the edges of the grass. It opens its wide mouth and pants up at me. It can't smile, but it does not roar.

*

Warning: Many days you will walk and walk and see nothing new. Many days you will do nothing but leave a trail of your own skin cells like bread crumbs for dust mites.

*

All summer, I felt like a big walking bag of chemicals. Science-minded friends reminded me that we are all big bags of chemicals, but so much time and effort had gone into balancing my chemicals that I felt the swish of them keeping my heart beating, my brain working, the words scrolling past my eyes and making sense. I walked every day. I rested every day. At the end of July, I had a cup of coffee and didn't break out in a cold sweat. Emboldened, I wrote an article. I held my breath when it went to press and didn't obsess when it was published. In August, I told a colleague that I had cracked up over the summer; I chose this phrase carefully because it best described what had happened to me. I developed a crack in my world view;

I was cracked open; better to crack up than to break down. She couldn't have been more understanding, because as it turned out, so had she. In September, I Zoom-taught my regular course load. That term, much was not perfect, including me.

In the end, I lost nine weeks of 2020 to the Attack of Reptile Brain, and I count myself lucky. Pandemic restrictions didn't cause my season of panic attacks, but they aligned with my trauma history and the sense of careening doom many people felt that spring. Walking helps to balance the unbearable, and this balance is delicate. Trauma survivors who are required to perform intense emotional labour, in the academy and elsewhere, need the ground beneath our feet. We need time alone where we don't have to explain anything to the creek or the fallen tree; we need to see that birds fly and rabbits run from us because they know about self-preservation. Neither *en garde* or subject to grade, this kind of walking is not about fitness or even that elusive scholarly work-life balance; it's about the hard, daily work of being present in the body I have now. It's the long work of giving space to what endures and is not inferno.

Daphne in Lockdown

Does she miss me tromping through, all my *oooh look at that?* Sometimes she'd like me to see the fourteen ways she fattened a flock of waxwings on hawthorn berries in February, but that is not the same as permission to walk all over her. She serves up cold dews, surprise garter snakes, a barred owl that scared the crap out of me when he swooped silent overhead. She is bigger than the yellow caution tape across the road: *access forbidden during pandemic.* She will command each doe to bear twins next May, urge snapping turtles to surface in the reservoir like bone submarines, let the kingfisher gorge herself to azure. Birch, please. She's always wanted to direct.

Daphne at Laurel Creek

Cold creek water and spring peepers: the river's daughter turned to tree. All it took was one lead-tipped arrow, and now there's a nymph who wants her own life. She knows her long division; she's the remainder. The abacus behind her eyes counts the geometric progression of berries that will oil the tight-wound sciatic nerves of poets, those who will chew the leaves into a fine stink-paste to tell the future. But Gaia save us from these pouty boys, when the god of reason becomes the grubby-handed patron saint of *baby, you're so fine*. Hey, sonny Apollo: Don't strip her leaves. Don't wear her out or on your head. Don't grab her glabrous leaves like they're some kind of a brass ring. She will burn the circumference of that wreath into your skull, a tonsure of acid. She sees you, circlet jerk, and she's adding you up on her branches. She'll turn you into a baccalaureate bastard impaled on the shrieks of red-winged blackbirds faster than you can say "Phoebus."

Daphne in Solidarity

There's always someone who thinks they own you,
thinks they decide for you, can trace where you are and
name you, dam you, reserve you, bury you, feed you
garbage and blame you. I'll call you water, if you call me land.

Collegial

A Survey

If you travel for work, and your colleague knocks on the door to your room and proposes a walk, do you say yes or decline politely?

If you decline the offer to walk, this survey is finished. Thank you for your participation.

If you say yes, wear your comfortable shoes. Take your room key and phone.

When you meet the others in the lobby, keep a close eye on the guy pacing back and forth like he's got ants in his pants, and take a moment to consider his definition of a walk and yours.

- ☐ Will he pursue an after-dinner walk like it's a chance to crush the miles and his competition?
- ☐ Is he a loud-laughing, backslapping shouter of a guy, smart enough but very devoted to the performance of his prowess?
- ☐ Do you think this description is too specific? If so, stop now and define, for yourself, the kind of colleague who just won't stop performing their position in a group. When your description is complete, continue.

As you head out, are you paired off by gender? By lengthening strides? Now is the time to keep an eye on the social dynamics of walking together or walking "together."

- ☐ After you pass through a parking lot, onto a major street and down a residential block, does he keep up a brisk pace, shouting questions back at you and then striding ahead without waiting for the answers?
- ☐ When you reach the end of several blocks and it's now full dark and he wants to plunge into a copse of trees, taking a thin trail through the underbrush, stop and listen to the river churning just beyond the trees. Can you tell if it is wider than the river you grew up with? Do you know where the trees end and the current begins?

If he peels off his jacket and turns to the rest of you, yelling, "This is where it gets interesting! Let's go!" then ask yourself:

- ☐ Do you want to enter some *Lord of the Flies*/*The Secret History* scenario?
- ☐ Are you officially over wanting to be the cool girl?
- ☐ Are you so aware of his privilege that it's like another person standing beside you?

This officially ends the survey. Your participation is appreciated and your confidentiality may be maintained. If you are willing to consider in-person activities and longer answers, please continue.

Possible questions to explore in breakout group discussion:
1. When you say, "Okay, have fun. I'm heading back," do the rest of your colleagues sigh and roll their eyes? Gloss, if you can, the tenor of that eye roll. Ask them to repeat it until you can describe it.
2. Role-play a scenario in which one member of the group says bitterly, "Oh and now I'm just expected to go back with you, right?" What is your reaction, and why?

Essay question: In 250 words or less, write a walk with co-workers in which everyone is cared for.

The conference is held close to a marsh with a boardwalk, and I cross the marsh every morning to get to the conference venue. My hotel serves terrible coffee from a church-basement urn, but the morning walk through the waterfowl park is everything. I watch a muskrat for five minutes one day and am late for the first meeting. I don't care. At the final night's banquet, someone on my right says, "We should go for a walk." I turn to the person on my left and say, "We're going for a walk." Five of us button our coats and walk out into the night, toward the boardwalk. We stop to get a retriever who needs an evening walk. It's dark, and we confer before entering the shelter of the treed path. We are a group. Anyone who can't see well? *Yes.* Put them in the centre of the group, with a guide. Anyone know this route? Two of our group have walked it for years – they're in charge of safety. The dog is in charge of modelling happiness. We take each other's hands and move forward onto the dark path, listening to the slap-slap of water lapping the shore, and then our feet are treading the worn boards. We whisper. The moon comes out and suddenly we are in the light, holding hands and looking up. The water glitters and something jumps, making rings. *This* is where it gets interesting.

Veil, Valley, Viaduct

A beautiful fall morning in Toronto: I gathered with fifteen women at St. Matthew's Clubhouse at the south end of Riverdale Park. We were there to walk into the Don River Valley. The ravine had long established a space for cycling with a paved trail, and the walking trails were becoming more developed and more popular. But fitness was not our goal. Though many of us were writers, more importantly for this walk, we were citizen scientists, birdwatchers, feminists and history and urban geography enthusiasts. We wanted to see the river valley as something more than what came between Castle Frank Station and Broadview Station on the Bloor subway line. As a bonus, this was a Poetry Walk in which the official "River Poets" of the Lost Rivers project read what they had written for and to the river. I walked with the others and had that experience of seeing a familiar thing in an unfamiliar way; in my twenties, this neighbourhood had been my old stomping grounds. Since then, I had lived in several other Canadian cities and finally landed 115 kilometres west of Toronto, in Waterloo – so near and yet so far.

The river walk was organized and led by Helen Mills, founder of Lost Rivers and a historian who had been working with the watershed of creek systems throughout the city since 1995. We stopped at several locations to discuss the history of the river, the people who lived beside it, its fluxes and redirections, the ravine's flora and fauna. We paused to hear the poems. A heavy rainstorm the night before had left the river swollen, and one of the first things we needed to check was whether or not it had burst its banks and flooded out the path. It hadn't, but it was a near thing – the water rushed by only inches beneath banks that didn't look especially substantial. Helen told us of the man who ran a ferry across the Don before the viaduct was built, and that John Graves Simcoe had renamed the river after the River Don in Yorkshire, and that its Anishinaabe name, Wonscotanach – "burning bright point" – was starting to gain wider use. We walked south, turning our backs to the Prince Edward Viaduct upon which pedestrians, cars and subways travelled over the Don Valley's ravine and river, and over us on its walking paths. I had history with that viaduct.

*

Vie-a-duck-t. Via meaning road and duct from ducere: the verb to lead in Latin. A viaduct differs from a bridge in that it leads a roadway or railway over a valley or low-lying area. According to the Online Etymological Dictionary, British landscape gardener Humphry Repton was the first to use the word viaduct in print, in 1816, describing "a form of bridge adapted to the purposes of passing over, which may unite strength with grace, or use with beauty." A bridge, more prosaically, is a structure designed to span physical obstacles. To non-architects (like me), it seems a fine distinction, in which beauty plays a part along with the idea of leading, drawing the traffic or railcars over a vast space beneath. The beauteous road that leads you over the unknown.

The Prince Edward Viaduct was designed by Edmund W. Burke and completed in 1918, but it is more famously understood to be a passion project of Toronto's commissioner of public works, R.C.

Harris, who lobbied hard for its necessity. It is more commonly known as the Bloor Street Viaduct, a geographical marker that you are either entering or leaving Toronto's east end, the place where the twenty-five-kilometre stretch of Bloor Street becomes Danforth Avenue. Does Danforth Avenue begin at the western edge of the viaduct or the eastern? The viaduct seems neither street nor venue but 100 percent itself: a transitional space between two parts of a sprawling city. The space under the viaduct, however, is forty metres of air above the green river valley, and a reminder that the viaduct carves out space below as much as above.

*

Come west several blocks for this piece of the story. Come west to the corner of Yonge and Bloor, and to a summer evening in the late 1990s. My friend and I stood outside the subway stop. We had just seen a movie, and while I don't remember which one, I can say for certain that I felt a little high on that feeling of being chock-full of cinema: ebullient and lighthearted. Coming out of a movie theatre to the contrast of the steamy honking bustle of that corner, we could see Toronto lighting up with its easy delights: patios, people dressed to impress and a million beauties laid out at our feet. We were young, and it was the kind of night that confirmed to each of us why we had moved to the big city. My friend's day had been long and she was ready to call it a night, so we were both headed home. The air tasted like possibility, and though my friend turned for the subway, I decided to walk. It was summer, a beautiful evening slowly fading into night, and I wanted to walk for at least a subway stop, maybe even the whole way home.

I did this a lot, dizzy with my anonymity and the elegance of solitude. Walking east on Bloor would take me past St. James' Cemetery, through the beginnings of the ravine around Castle Frank

Station, past the high school where I used to take a poetry workshop through continuing education – a workshop from which I used to float home over the Bloor Street Viaduct, giddy with how words worked. Forty metres above the valley, I could see the lines of cars lit up on the parkway and the deep darkness of the ravine. Walking in Toronto meant having an obscured view a lot of the time, and I loved the viaduct for its city view with big sky, day or night. From the viaduct's other end, it was three blocks home, to my place where I wrote late into the night and got up for work the next day tired but happy. It made my day job bearable.

This was a great route home, full of lots of my favourite spots in that part of the city. The Bloor Street Viaduct will always remind me of an episode near the start of Michael Ondaatje's *In the Skin of a Lion*, about Harris's drive to get the viaduct built to join the two parts of the city, about the ceremonial opening of the structure and about an accident that happened during its opening. The book blends fiction and history – the story of the young nun who was blown off the bridge by high winds that caught the folds of her habit and dropped her over the side is fictional. In the novel, the nun falls through space and is caught by the arm by a worker strung up on a pulley on one of the structure's beams, a carpenter putting finishing touches on the truss arches. No one sees him catch her, and he gets her to safety. Together, they make a sling for his shoulder, dislocated in the act of catching her, from the cloth of her nun's veil. She recovers and, presumed dead, begins a new life with a new name. When I was in my twenties and had just moved to Toronto, the story of the nun seemed so profoundly parallel with my own experience of moving away from my restrictive family to a city where I was anonymous and training to make art. The story was a favourite of mine for years. When I moved to the east end and crossed the viaduct twice a day or more, I thought of that story every time.

In Ondaatje's novel, R.C. Harris despairs when he sees the nun fall off the edge of the viaduct, buffeted by high winds. Describing the viaduct as Harris's child (that is, a favourite project that Harris had championed for years), Ondaatje writes: "His child was not even an hour old, and it was already a murderer." Despite the fact that the story of the nun was Ondaatje's invention, in reality as many as five hundred people between 1918 and 2003 chose the viaduct as their spot to die, launching themselves into the space above the valley. Eventually, the City of Toronto installed the steel rods of the Luminous Veil to deter jumpers. But when I walked it often in the 1990s, it was veil-less: just me, concrete and sky.

*

Back at Bloor and Yonge, the sun was low and my friend boarded the subway heading west. I set off east, the night crawling into bloom before me. I could smell lilacs, for sure, and maybe catalpas as I passed the cemetery. Walking twelve blocks home was nothing. I had done it a hundred times, first because I wanted to see things, then because I was saving money, and now for the pure pleasure of my feet in motion while the dark is drawn across the city like a quilt. I was heading home to the lush garden, my wooden patio among the tall trees and my rooms full of books.

I missed the moment he sidled up and started talking like he knew me – a stranger who'd fallen in beside me just as I left the last blocks of stores and patios behind me; as trees began to hang over the sidewalk, sometimes blocking out the streetlights. At first he was all chatter – "How are you tonight," and "Great night for walking," and "Where you going?" – and I thought I would outwalk him if I just kept going, that there were a thousand people in bars he could flirt with instead, that my walking was dull, that I was dull, that I would not stop and he'd be bored by me. But he kept stride with me even though I was taller, and gradually he started to talk less, which made me talk more. The only thing worse than walking and talking with a strangely menacing man into a completely quiet area with no cabs, no pedestrians and lots of dark spaces is doing all of that in silence. I pictured the blocks ahead, the quiet spots where the dense brush of Rosedale Valley encroached on the north side of Bloor.

We passed the eastern entrance to Sherbourne Station, a token-entry-only gate with a steep set of outdoor stairs that was barely lit: *Oh hell no.* We passed Castle Frank Station, its only entrance on the north side of the street, across five lanes of traffic. Couldn't get to it. He could drag me into the start of the ravine. I calculated the amount of force he'd need to exert divided by my height times his mass minus the element of surprise. I calculated while I talked and talked. I had the added challenge of talking without saying anything about myself, nothing about where or how I lived. I shot the shit like it was mine to shoot. His conversation was not especially engaging, or maybe it was and I was just distracted by trying not to die.

The truth is that I don't remember much about my unwanted companion; he was shorter than me, stocky, swarthy as though he could have been Greek or Italian. He spoke affably. He told me that he ran a gaming business, and I asked what that was. He laughed and kept saying, "You don't know what gaming is? I can't believe it! You don't know?" But he never defined it. I asked if it was gambling, and he laughed harder and said, "I don't believe it!" some more.

The Bloor Street Viaduct reared up ahead. It marked the last lonely stretch before lights and patios and open stores and crowds of people. If I could make it across, I could lose him. A former instructor said that whenever she rode the subway east and the train broke out of the underground tunnel and into the light above the valley, she took the visual as a reminder to count her blessings.

Then he asked, "Hey, could I use your phone?" It was the early 1990s. There were no cellphones. He meant he wanted to use the phone at *my house.* There was no goddamned way that was going to happen; I was going to lose this guy as soon as we got to Broadview. But I couldn't let him know that, so I chirped, "Sure!" like I was a girl stupid enough to think this was a mild request. We stepped out onto the viaduct, its concrete railings only rib-high.

I tried to count my blessings: (1) still alive, (2) still talking, (3) still moving toward the lights of safety, (4) still alive.

By the second half of the viaduct, I began just saying whatever popped into my head. I narrated for my stalker the opening pages of *In the Skin of a Lion*: the ribbon-cutting ceremony, the young nun, the wind, her fall and mid-air rescue by the Macedonian carpenter. My stalker flinched and his face took on an unreadable expression. *Oh god*, I thought, *that's how he'll kill me; he'll just lift me over the side and drop me into the valley and there will be no one to catch me.*

But he didn't. The creepy little smile he'd been wearing from the start dropped from his face and he asked, "Did that happen?" I said, "Yes, of course," because Ondaatje's fiction was more believable than whatever I'd been gibbering on about for blocks. I needed the story to be intriguing enough to cover the journey across the viaduct. He looked astounded, and I thought, too late, *Damn! This story's too good, now he'll hang around wanting to know the end and I'll be some twentieth-century Scheherazade spending 1001 nights with this bastard. Fuck, fuck, fuck.* We stepped off the east end of the viaduct and neared the crowds on the Danforth. I had exactly five more minutes in which to lose him.

And out of the crowd, like a vision, my friend David appeared. David, from the Hebrew *Dawid*, meaning "beloved." He was on his way home from buying something. Groceries? Clothes? I only remember he was carrying a bag. Just like that, it was over. As soon as David saw me and stopped to talk, the stalker faded away, melted into the crowd. I said to David, "Come with me, I need to buy you a drink RIGHT NOW." He seemed a little puzzled by my account of the ordeal but was glad to have helped.

For years, I've wondered if my stalker was just a sad jerk who thought this was a way to pick up chicks, or if he was as weirdly menacing as I thought. In the end, it doesn't matter. He scared the shit out of me, and he knew it and liked it. I used the story of the nun to stun him, used the viaduct's breadth and vista and fable to distract him. The story shifted from women who could fall off a bridge and disappear to women who lived, who sat in small rooms later that night and counted the ways they were still alive.

*

In her book *Feminist City: A Field Guide*, Leslie Kern notes that women's fear of violence from men manifests as a fear of spaces where we might be attacked, and that we live our lives avoiding spaces because it is functionally impossible to avoid men. She also notes that even when we live our lives boldly, we often refuse to acknowledge that we make good choices and savvy decisions, that we protect ourselves well, that we figure out the best strategy to get through hard situations. Instead we say, "That was stupid. I was so lucky to live through that. I'll never walk there again."

So I won't say that.

In 2019, twenty-five years after I was stalked, and 101 years after the viaduct was opened, I travelled the two hours to the Don Valley to walk it with a different group of women. This time I was in the lead as we crossed the pedestrian bridge at the south end of River-view Park. We turned north and crossed the river again, heading toward and then beneath the viaduct. The river was quiet, and we were looking for a sculpture installation I had read about, Cree artist Duane Linklater's *Monsters for Beauty, Permanence and Individuality*. When we found it, installed beside the pedestrian path so people can come upon it unaware, we stopped to walk among Linklater's stylized gargoyles, fallen to earth with the viaduct's arches and trusses looming in the background, its tracks and roads growling with traffic. There was a female sculpture among the gargoyles, a woman bent over in a crouch, her veiled head obscuring her face unless you knelt down and peered up at her. I stood by the stone nun who hid her face and looked up into the forty metres of space beneath the viaduct, getting older and feeling bold.

Take Back the Night

Take back the night to where it began, where it emerged wet and wriggling from between its mother's thighs, Mistress of Sleep and Keeper of the Hours. Take back the night like a book from the library: *here are the blank minutes between nine and six, here is the dream from which you sat bolt upright, sorry these nightmares are overdue.* Take back the night like your empties: recycle and retrieve your deposit.

Take back what you said, take it back to the start. Take back your mink, take back your pearls. Take back what you borrowed, take back what you lent. What made you think? I was one of those girls. Take back is not talkback, backtalk goes with take luck, fake-like and fucked-up, talk ink and think Locke. Or Kant. What made you? Think. I was one. Those girls. Lark and look. Lake and tank. Thank you. Lake you. Like you. Take it to the lost and found.

I thought he was calling to make me take it back. I sewed my lips shut. I thought he was writing to fake me lake it slack. I mowed my lawn shut. I thought he was falling to take me make it lack. I toed the line shut. I knew he was friending to slake his lack. Oh muck. Oh unapologetic suck. Blunt skunk, hank of fur, slinking back. You didn't think time would last so long. A mind is a terrible funk. Take back the knight, take back your fight, talk back to your overbite. I know you: What made you? Think one of those girls. Right.

Syrinx

The birds were triggered at dawn. They sang to Leonardo until he freed them. They banded Audubon to see if he'd return. They wrote to John Clare on their eggs: postage due. They spoke Greek to Virginia, told Rosa Luxemburg of revolutionary clouds. The crows made a tiny paper Joseph Cornell and put him in a box. The ravens say, *You lookin' at me? I don't see anyone else here.* The finches want to see some credentials. The sparrows insist on their standards; they are not speaking to the starlings. The pigeons found it hard to tell the truth to Flannery O'Connor and hard to tell lies about Frank McCourt. The albatross was in on that necktie party from the start. Birds don't believe in big government or omertà. We showed them the video, and when they saw that deer swallow a chickadee, they were as shocked as anyone.

Vigil

Get outside, they said. *Walk for your physical and mental health*, they said. *Enjoy the beautiful weather, it'll be winter soon enough.* It's winter now, even though it's June 2021.

*

On June 6, four members of a Muslim Pakistani Canadian family – the Afzaals – were murdered while they were walking in a green area in London, Ontario, a city just up the 401 from where I live. Four people are dead because a young man mowed them down with his car: grandmother Talat Afzaal, mother Madiha Salman, father Salman Afzaal and their teenaged daughter, Yumna. Islamophobia is prevalent, and these murders are stark and horrible reminders that safety is extremely relative. The everyday walk is a unit of danger; the everyday can be violent depending on what body you occupy. I think of the members of the Afzaal family, breathing in the fresh air and being good citizens of Pandemic Canada, walking as the prime minister himself advised when they were killed by a racist twenty-year-old.

The very next day, as the region was reeling from this act of violence, another assault occurred that did not make the national news. A man sexually assaulted a woman on a popular walking trail in my neighbourhood, one I frequent – a pleasant tree-lined trail with good spots for birdwatching and a creek running through it. The trail skirts the creek bed and runs behind a row of houses, each with spacious backyards full of decks and treehouses and playground equipment. That trail – signs proudly proclaiming it part of the Trans Canada Trail – is where I first saw goldfinches returning to the neighbourhood after several years' absence. The trail runs through a slice of Carolinian forest, an environment that is rapidly disappearing from the region but which many are fighting to preserve. I've seen red-bellied and red-headed woodpeckers there a few times, and downy and hairy woodpeckers regularly, along with cardinals, blue jays, cedar waxwings, sparrows, juncos, crows and the ubiquitous chickadees. I walked there last Christmas Day, passing families in masks and walking under a stand of cedars one of the neighbours had bedecked with blue lights and silver balls. I wonder if I passed the rapist that day, if he nodded to me and noted I was alone as I wished him the best of the season, the way my father always did when I walked with him: looking everyone in the eye and greeting them with a smile.

I learned about the sexual assault only because I had subscribed to the NextDoor email/social media app for the surrounding area. I don't visit the newsfeed much but check in sometimes for mild and quirky hyper-local news, like who wants ground-cover plants, where the neighbourhood foxes are living and bird identification requests. That morning, however, the headline "Sexual Assault on Neighbourhood Trail" shoved everything else out of my mind. The usual happened, replies came pouring in: shock and outrage, disbelief that our seemingly safe neighbourhood could be the site of such violence. And then the caveats: "Please be vigilant neighbours while walking!"; "Please don't go out alone day or night." The back of my mouth tasted sour and when I lifted my hands to type a reply, I felt so ground down by the same conversation, by the same well-meaning-but-misguided people that my brain fog rolled in thick and fast. I don't know how I could be more vigilant when out walking, except of course to stay inside. That would be vigilant, but it wouldn't be walking. I was grateful to see one woman pipe up: "It's up to the women to be trapped and afraid and not go out alone. Somehow it always ends up on the women." I'm glad she wrote it, and I couldn't have said it better myself. I don't always walk alone, but I often do in order to clear my head, to look quietly at things and to feel the beauty of solitude.

When I told a colleague about this, she said, "What if in every spot where there had been a sexual assault, there was a memorial or a sign, like some people do for traffic accidents, saying 'This happened here'?" My first thought was that I'd like to see that, not to scare people but to remind us that *we* make the neighbourhood, that safety is something to work for, that we need to put our discomfort on the line. Poet Moez Surani is currently working on a project called "Some Contemporary Sites of Islamophobia" where he posts photos of apparently banal spaces. So far I've seen Moez post photos of a gas station, a busy urban street in front of a bank and a grocery store. The dullness of these spaces, how they could be anywhere in any North American city, is the point: violence wants us to believe that its extremities make it special, but it happens everywhere.

The second thought I had regarding my colleague's question was that if there were signs everywhere to mark sexual assaults, then we wouldn't be able to move for their density. They would pile up in dorm rooms and hotels, on streets and in library stacks, in banquet halls and restaurant kitchens and sports fields and schools. The nation we call Canada is built on the blood of Indigenous people – those signs would not only be everywhere; they would be seven generations deep. Properly marked graveyards of Indigenous children who attended residential schools would be one kind of sign, to locate the violence, to broadcast it, to name the children. Formal charges would be another kind of sign, to name and prosecute the perpetrators.

There are handmade signs up on one part of the trail, signs I spotted weeks before the report of the assault. I was out foraging wildflowers to make ink – an ongoing personal chemistry project at which I am intermittently successful. I'd leaned my bike against a tree and was moving up and down the trail looking for wildflowers, working back and forth with the app on my phone to identify them. I was not looking up or stopping to check my surroundings. I was doing what information-obsessed people do while out in the woods: looking out for stuff. But close to a patch of forget-me-nots, I saw a large cardboard sign tied with care to one of the trees. It was cut in a zigzag pattern to look like the sun, and on its orange surface was written, "That fuzzy, warm feeling when you do something nice for someone – chase it." Further down the trail, there was a second handmade sign, the same shape but in bright yellow: "Hope, Pray, and Don't Worry."

Other than the rapist, the woman he attacked and the police, no one knows exactly where the attack took place. The report in the newspaper noted the trail but not the specific section of the trail. I have no idea whether the signs are near the place where the rapist assaulted the woman, but I read the homemade trail signs differently after hearing of the assault. What seemed quirky and a bit naive before news of the attack seems creepy in retrospect, especially that imperative to "chase it!" It seems unlikely that the rapist put up the signs, but twenty-twenty hindsight is brutal when you wake up to it. Admonitions to hope and love are as wispy as smoke when they decorate a site of violence, and the advice itself, to go after what you want, can for some mean assaulting and killing people who are out walking. The whole trail glows toxic.

News of the assault vanished from the news cycle within

twenty-four hours. The assaulter was caught and held in custody. There was no news of the woman, as there never is, not even a report on her health. I know why; the result is that she is not all right and won't be for a long time, and we don't have a sign for that. Some of us can "get outside and enjoy the day," and some of us can cower in our houses. I am a little scared, but I'm a lot angry and I want to go to the trail and wrestle it back to my side. I want to wear my big boots in the sweltering summer heat and stomp up and down that trail, leaving giant dinosaur footprints. I notice, too, my reluctance to do just that. I can feel the admonitions working within me. Stay inside or be extra vigilant. I am vigilant; men should be less rapey.

*

Vigilant (fifteenth century): from the Latin verb *vigilare*, from *vigil* – "keeping awake." The grammarian in me wants to shout about the importance of the present particle here. It signifies the continuous present: that which is being done perpetually, always in the action of doing. We are keeping awake all the time. The Proto-Indo-European root of *vigilant* is *weg*, meaning "to be strong or lively," which seems to me very different from staying awake anxiously or carefully. It's much bolder to be strong or lively in the case of threat.

Sometimes I think of scanning my route as I walk with my estrogen-fuelled heat-seeking vision, noting the positions of all other humans within my sight. This morning, I detected the glow of five other bodies: two kids drawing with sidewalk chalk on the northeast corner of the block, a neighbour who I know raking his lawn and an unknown male walker and his dog half a block behind me. I made my choices accordingly; I skirted around the kids to give them space to play, waved at my neighbour and kept one eye on the dog walker. When I saw this pseudo-technology in *RoboCop* (and later in the *Terminator* movies), the cyborg cop's visual scanning technique was immediately familiar to me. Admittedly, this kind of constant surveying is more difficult in a city, but women who live in cities do it a lot of the time. We look at who's coming toward us, who we are passing. We usually don't have the luxury of noodling along, oblivious.

This ability was amply demonstrated to me when I was a student. In a course on stage movement and theatrical combat, a staple in theatre study, the instructor conducted an exercise to illustrate how people perceive and react to danger intuitively – an important factor to know if you are in a staged fight. Our participation in the exercise was voluntary; we could opt out. I don't remember if anyone did.

The exercise was simple: The instructor stood at one end of our long practice room. A student stood at the other with their back turned, facing away from the instructor. The instructor began to move, slowly and silently, toward the student. When the student felt threatened, they said, "Stop," and the instructor stopped approaching them. The instructor did not carry a weapon; he was not a physically large person. He had been consistent and clear so far in his instruction and we had every reason to trust him in a well-lit room with twenty other students watching.

The idea was that students had to use their intuition or perception or whatever they could rely upon to feel the (manufactured) threat. The straight cis men in the class were reluctant to admit when they felt threatened, yet determined to show that they had the savvy to know when they should turn and fight. I could see some of them trying to listen for the instructor's movements, which were remarkably quiet. Those fellas had mixed results: some did okay, some had no idea. For them, despite having likely been threatened by other men at some point in their lives, this exercise was a puzzler and their hit-and-miss results showed their confusion. But the women and the queer men were not confused at all; nearly every one of us scored high on the awareness meter. The instructor varied his timing, sometimes waiting before beginning his approach, sometimes starting right away. The women and queer guys weren't listening for his approach; we were feeling for it with every molecule of our backs and legs, reaching into the space between us and the instructor, and sensing when he moved. "Stop," we said, one by one. "Stop." "Stop."

Our straight cis male peers were as aghast as they were impressed; they couldn't figure it out. It's important to remember that with the exception of the instructor, we were all between nineteen and twenty-three years old. The women already knew how to sense an attacker (even a fake one) while the (straight cis) men had no idea how. The instructor took the opportunity to say, "Guys, the women know because their lives depend on it. Never sneak up on a woman, not even as a joke." It would be another ten years before I heard, in public, discussions on how male allies could assist women by building awareness about how women used public spaces. In other words, keep your distance.

I look back on this exercise with chagrin. While I appreciated that it woke men in the class to women's daily vigilance, and I liked how the instructor addressed this lack of education in men's lives, I shake my head at the classroom reproduction of a manufactured threat for women – that we all stood, one by one, in front of our peers, and demonstrated our intimate fear of violence. Each of us showcased our fight, freeze or flight tendencies in the split-second after we said, "Stop." Some of us whirled around, some of us stiffened our backs and didn't move, a few of us leapt forward like rabbits the moment we said it. To the instructor's credit, he stopped every single time. Though he had created the situation, he kept his word that we would control it. He didn't lurch forward, pretending to grab us, and then make a joke of our fear. We all know one of those guys, maybe several.

The threat of violence made women lifelong social distancers and consistent negotiators of social spaces long before (and continuing well after) pandemic restrictions. And speaking of chagrin, I too have startled a woman in the woods. I walked up from an angle she wasn't expecting, and even though I did not get near her, she panicked and ran when she saw me. My gender might have been obscured, or maybe it didn't matter to her. The flush of frightening another human being whooshed through me: surprise, shame. I nearly called, "It's okay! It's just me!" which would have made no sense to anyone.

*

In her book *Treed*, Ariel Gordon writes about a man she calls "the Forest Perv," a serial masturbator who frequented Winnipeg's Assiniboine Forest for a while, appearing just off the path, naked and busy and designedly visible to women walkers. She and I are walking that same path when she reminds me to keep an eye out, because he was never caught. We're on a known path, but there were only a few other cars in the lot and we haven't seen anyone in twenty minutes. I recall the last public masturbator I saw, in Lisbon, on the walk up the steep streets in the Alfama district leading to the Castelo de São Jorge, my colleague chatting beside me while a dog took a very wet shit on the cobbled street in front of us. An older man turned toward us with his dick in his hand. I was instantly furious; I glared at him, calculating. He wasn't that big, and I could – and would – take him in a fight. My adrenaline roared up my back until I saw he also looked elderly and addled – by dementia, most likely. I turned away. "That's disgusting!" my colleague yelled and I turned to discover her pointing at the dog shit. I hustled us away into the ancient fortress with its peacocks and only told her about the masturbator later. The dog had taken all her attention; she didn't even notice the man with his dick out. "You're kidding," she kept saying over lunch.

That may be a poor comparison, however. The Forest Perv and

his ilk are less benign than Sad Alfama Dick. In 2018, some guy – a young man the age of my students – tried to attack a woman walking by herself at twilight in the Assiniboine Forest. He ran at her shouting, but she didn't run; she faced him head-on and tripped him. He then threw himself at her legs, which is when she punched him and called the police while he lay there moaning in pain. I don't know if she yelled for him to stop. The police came right away and the thwarted attack made the papers. That article was a satisfying read; I was glad to hear of her competence and her anger. I thought too of the young man and wondered what he thought he was doing. I didn't wonder long. I'd known my abuser as a young man, and knew that scaring people was one of his greatest pleasures, that he would plan elaborate set-ups to frighten women and then call it a joke. He would lovingly tell these stories, over and over again – how one woman screamed in terror, how another tried to hit him. All the while he laughed and insisted it was just a joke. I have no evidence that the young man who tried to attack the woman in the Assiniboine Forest was like my abuser, though I didn't waste a lot of time wondering about his mindset. I focused instead on the distance between what he thought would happen and what did.

*

"The price of freedom is eternal vigilance" is a statement famously misattributed to Thomas Jefferson, who was himself a rapist (just ask Sally Hemings) and slave owner, so whether or not he wrote it, I am not taking his word on the price of freedom. For this statement to be true, Jefferson would have to keep awake *to watch himself.*

The price of freedom – so heavily debated in 2020 and 2021 as some claimed the right not to wear a mask and not to be vaccinated – and the history of public safety depends on not only where you are but who's on watch. (Why is freedom a commodity, to be maintained at a cost?) To be vigilant is to watch: How could a man sexually assault a woman so close to these suburban houses? Where was this community that's supposed to be "caring for each other" because "we're all in this together"? Were people so busy hoping and praying that they didn't look out for women who use the trail? Did "don't worry" translate to "don't care"? Or are we all in this together except for the usual rules that say women, people of colour, queer people and Indigenous people need to do extra work to live safely in their own bodies?

On the day of the funeral for the four murdered members of the Afzaal family in London, news of the bones of Indigenous children found on the sites of three residential schools in Canada (with many more to come) dominated the airwaves. In the wake of this story, the single incident of assault in my neighbourhood was dwarfed by seven generations of genocide, including mass incarceration and mass pedophilia. Seeing so many people wearing orange and flying orange flags and posting orange signs in my neighbourhood made me think of those signs that do not exist, the signs that commemorate assault locations. It gave me the thinnest sliver of hope that we might be able to find a way to sit together in this vigil.

Studies in neuroergonomics shown that the stress of vigilance actually decreases the body's ability to maintain vigilance, especially when people are required to observe in circumstances where spatial uncertainty is or was part of the equation. That is, the more that we try to stay rigorously alert in a space that we don't control, the poorer the job we'll do because the body cannot maintain the level of performance we think it requires.

It took me three weeks to return to the trail, by which time it had ceased to be my trail. I felt itchy at the thought that I had ever claimed it. I took my bike and went there at high noon. I rode up and down the trail and saw no women walking alone. They were in pairs and small groups; everyone nodded politely and I did, too, though I wanted to scream. I did not stop to collect wild plants to make ink. The bright sun-shaped signs were nowhere to be seen, but as I exited onto the street, I passed the spray-painted tag on the community mailbox that says, "Thanks for everything today." I cycled up the hill, knowing that I may be passing the assaulted woman's house, or even the rapist's. I pedalled harder as the angle of the hill sloped upwards, willing the strongest part of my body, the long legs I grew before my eleventh birthday to power me home. Their musculature was built by decades of dancing, running, climbing, lifting, kicking. My legs are the engine, my lungs the bellows, my body the machinery of vigil.

A Feminist Guide
to Reservoirs

You want to but can't
scream at how
we're hated. But you

recall that herons stand
all day in stormwater
ponds, keep their distance

from other herons. This is not
meant to prove
but to say herons know

what you're missing.
You have long
suspected capitalism hates

women and geese crave
stormwater
and gender parity.

STRAGGLE

You thought you had made it,
battered but alive,
to the future. The river

is charged with all the artificial
sweeteners that pass
unaltered through our bodies,

down the sewers and into the river,
molecules of Coke
slipping down the geological

staircase into Lake Erie. Haldimand
Tract, six miles on
both sides of the river, Six Nations

land, and every white person
you know acts
so surprised. *Oh, I didn't*

know. One in three
women will
be sexually assaulted.

I was never taught that.
No one is, until
you are. A creek can

whisper through a city,
a rumour of water
that is water. You cannot

get your breath. Someone
spray-paints
I Am Broken on the bunker

over the culvert where
you watch mallards
emerge like a magic

act. You're not, or not
any more
than usual.

A Guide to "A Feminist Guide to Reservoirs"

In 2019, the City of Waterloo was ranked the most dangerous Canadian city for women to live in by the Canadian Council for Policy Alternatives. It had held this position since 2015. My hometown, Winnipeg, has long held the dubious status as the violent crime capital of Canada, which only proves that a geographical move is not a cure for what ails you – or for what could kill you.

Laurel Creek, named Little Beaver Creek by Mennonite and Lutheran settlers in the mid-1800s, flooded the township of Waterloo several times between the 1860s and 1960s. Around 1920, settlers began calling it Laurel Creek. In 2021, the Land Back Camp, a camp for Indigenous queer and Two-Spirit youth, relocated to the shore of the Laurel Creek Reservoir, seeking space that will be permanently designated as their own for ongoing ceremony and community. The Laurel Creek Watershed is located in the centre of the Grand River Watershed, and covers about 74.4 square kilometres, including tributaries of several other smaller creeks. And for the record, I've twice seen beavers in the creek, and more often seen evidence of beavers in the many gnawed-down saplings near the shore of the reservoir.

A friend once pointed out to me what he called the source of

Laurel Creek, a small bubbling spout in Sunfish Lake that shot off in a rivulet heading southeast. Though I've since discovered that the real source is farther north, I remember being surprised that a source could be pinpointed at all. Raised at the junction of two large rivers, I was a watershed naïf. But for the past decade, I have walked the creeks and tributaries of this watershed every week, sometimes by the shores of reservoirs and sometimes by the many other tributaries that surface throughout Waterloo and Kitchener, beside bike trails and through neighbourhoods. It took me a long time to discover even a fraction of how extensive this water system is – all these creeks, with their culverts and graffitied concrete canals, mallards and geese and muskrats and stands of staghorn sumac and Virginia creeper. I think about what walking in a wild but urbanized space means to my feminist practice, and what feminism has to do with land listening and decolonization – what it would mean to begin reconciliation with how we treat the land and the water.

Falling

A Reckoning

Your body is a space that sees.
– Lia Halloran

For the first winter I spent in Southwestern Ontario, I lived in a house with a long driveway that ran along one side. I don't remember what I was doing the night I fell on that icy driveway, but I do remember that my feet whisked out from under me, and then I was flat on my back, staring up at the night sky and the soffits of the house. I stayed there for a minute, knowing it was going to hurt to move, that I was going to have to get up carefully and inch along the driveway, get up the stairs of the porch and go inside and tell John that I fell: the hows, the whys, the be-carefuls. None of this was impossible, and I would eventually do it, but lying there on the ice, knowing I was hurt but not badly, it all seemed like too much. I was felled like a tree. I didn't want to move. I wanted to rest a minute before I had to get up and wade back into the humanness of having a body.

We fall in love, we fall asleep, we fall ill, we fall among thieves, we fall from grace.

I knew a boy in theatre school whose party trick was to fall down stairs. The day I met him, he performed this feat on the marble staircase of the main building – just chucked his compact self down the flight of stairs, rolled down them like a puppy, then stood and waited for me to be horrified, thrilled or both.

Safe to say, this party trick was also his pickup act.

My mother fell on the ice one November. Doing so was her greatest fear, but at the time, she was worried only about how to get to the hospital to visit my father, who was recovering from surgery. In an act of kindness that I wouldn't believe if I saw it in a film but am forever grateful for, a woman driving by saw my mother fall, stopped her car and drove my mother to the hospital, where she was assessed in Emergency and deemed badly bruised and shaken but basically fine. The nurses put my mother in a wheelchair and took her to the fourth floor to sit by my father's bedside. Eleven years later and at that same hospital, taking X-rays after my mother had fallen again, we discovered that she had broken her pelvis during that first fall. Buster Keaton is said to have broken every bone in his body, including his neck, but he too did not notice for three days. Mr. Keaton, may I introduce my mother? You two can compare notes.

*

I fell hard and gracelessly once at work, on a morning when the hallway floors had been waxed but not buffed. The tiles were like a Slip 'N Slide. I walked carefully, carefully, and was about ten yards from my office when I went down like a ton of bricks: purse, books, files and all. I was in a summer dress whose hem went everywhere. It was a most immodest fall.

*

If our bodies are spaces that see, sometimes our perspectives can suddenly be close to the ground. It can be very jarring to fall, psychologically as well as physically, especially if there's no special reason – no tree root to trip over, no crack in the sidewalk. It alters your world view; you are moving along safely in the world, and all of a sudden gravity is no longer your friend and the landscape is brand new. You wake to the idea that it is not safe to be unobservant, to saunter along thinking of other things. Alyson Hallett, in *Walking Stumbling Limping Falling,* makes the excellent point that being constantly mindful is exhausting on any walk, and that the mental and emotional labour that goes into avoiding falling makes us small. In my thirties, when I ran every day, I thought many times of Natalie Goldberg's story from *Wild Mind* about her irrational fear that if she ran too fast, she would outrun her own body's balance and fall. I recall this story because it seems odd and yet strangely possible. Running, or walking upright, proceeds on an implicit trust that you won't fall, a reliance on what is known as contrapposto, or counterpoise: the unconscious but vital bodily manoeuvring that allows human beings to shift their weight from foot to foot, and align their hips and knees and other joints to maintain balance. As a word for the miraculous, counterpoise entices but sometimes fails. If we are out in the world to experience our bodies in motion, to look, to hear, to collect data or just enjoy the day, hyperawareness is a hyper drag.

I fell on an ordinary downtown street on a bright summer evening in Vancouver. I was wearing flat shoes, and the street and sidewalk were awash in sunlight. I had just flown in that afternoon, and I was with my friend, walking to her favourite restaurant. I was so happy to be in Vancouver, out with my bestie with the whole evening in front of us, and then I was on the ground. From behind me, I heard someone yell, "Whoa! What a wipeout!"

The comic pratfall, though it is less popular now than it was when

I was growing up, when physical slapstick was a staple on TV variety shows, maintains a hold on the public imagination. The man who was arguably the twentieth century's greatest physical comedian, Charlie Chaplin, started his career doing a comic drunk act on the British music hall circuit, performing in the persona of a rickety elderly man. This was music hall tradition; a young man falling over was one kind of laugh, but the comic possibilities of a creaky body with an uncertain step has been well-understood (and even craved) by audiences at least since commedia dell'arte. The uncertain body, the body that may move erratically or stiffly, occupies the space of concern and comedy. Think of Tim Conway as the shuffling old man on *The Carol Burnett Show* in the 1960s and 1970s. Slipping on a banana peel or a waxed floor may inspire a sympathetic reaction rather than a laugh, but a sudden loss of uprightness, a rapid concession to gravity is odd enough – and often swift enough – to be funny. In the early twentieth century, Henri Bergson famously wrote that laughter is sparked by "a certain mechanical inelasticity" that occurs "where one would expect to find the wide-awake adaptability and the living pliableness of a human being." In other words, when the flexible human body acts with unexpected mechanical rigidity.

That summer evening in Vancouver, my friend didn't see me fall. She turned to me in mid-remark and I was not at her side. She looked over her shoulder to see if I had stopped to look in a store window – nope. Then she looked down, and there I was, on the sidewalk, looking as though I had been dropped from the sky. In my case, my friend didn't laugh, but I get it, it was a comic moment. I was walking, and then I was sprawled in an awkward half-split. Scary for the body and funny for the mind.

The cause for my fall was embarrassingly simple. My right foot skidded on a patch of gravel and just kept going. At the shout from behind me – "What a wipeout!" – I wondered, *Why does this always happen to me?*, then said, "I'm all right," and started to struggle to my feet to assess the damage. I was less hurt than disappointed in what seemed like my perpetually adolescent position, rising and brushing myself off, assuring everyone that I was okay, wondering if the ripped knee in my trousers was salvageable and knowing that I would be limping into the restaurant with dirty hands, torn trousers and a bloody knee like a twelve-year-old who had just slid into third base. I was forty and I had just tripped over dust.

The person who'd called out from behind me wasn't mocking me; I heard the concern in her voice, that this was no ordinary wipe-out but an adult woman crashing to the ground on a city street. I liked that the expression hearkened back to one I used all the time as a kid, when my friends and I would fall off our bikes or collide with the ice while skating. It was a weekly occurrence and a point of pride: "Man, I wiped out so hard on Sunday at the rink. I tripped and went flying. You should have seen it!" This point of pride has a lot to do with the resilience of active young bodies for whom abrasions (road rash or "plaid knees") are merely part of biking, skating, running, gymnastics and a dozen other activities. To fall in this context was evidence you were out there taking risks – learning to ride your bike with no hands, or doing a flying camel on skates. To fall was to hurt yourself briefly, with the pleasure of admiring the bruise later.

But then you get older. I remember when a fellow student came to class the day after he had been in an accident. The car he and four others were riding in rolled over twice in a ditch off the highway. Miraculously, no one was hurt, and he laughed as he told the class, giddy with survival or young enough to think of this as just one more adolescent wipeout. The professor waited until he had finished his story and then she said four words in the voice of an oracle: "You are mortal, child." I can still hear her say it, that pronouncement of mortality rattling around in my skull. The knowledge that you are mortal leads to admiring your own wipeouts a lot less.

My fall in Vancouver was awkwardly ridiculous; my right leg had stuck straight out in front of me while my left leg twisted behind me. And I imagine it was shocking to those who saw it: Did someone push me? Was my leg broken? Was I drunk? (No, no and no.) Wiping out didn't seem to happen to other adults, but there I was, bleeding and wondering when I would be adult enough to not fall down in the street. The answer is not yet and maybe never. So I was relieved to read UK-based professor Mike Michael's chapter about the misstep as a "research event": that is, an event in adult life during which the moment before the fall, the act of falling and the recovery from the fall offer us ways to think through our locomotion, our relationship to gravity and even falling as a physical ability.

One of the things that Michael discusses is the misstep as a "social threat"; others around the faller may wilfully ignore the event or pay what he calls "civil inattention" to the person who has fallen. Michael notes that this instinct may be to spare the dignity of the faller – because, as my mother always said, "It's rude to stare." But Michael suggests there may be another motivation. Ignoring the fall maintains the observer's status as someone who has NOT fallen, someone stable, secure, grounded. I'm intrigued that Michael notes this as a class distinction. To fall is to lose control and to have that loss of control amply demonstrated in public. Little kids, drunk or stoned people, old people and disabled people fall; people who aren't paying attention, people who have temporarily lost their ability to pay attention and people whose physical body forces them to pay significantly *more* attention to their locomotion sometimes fall. This metaphor can be transposed to logical and verbal missteps in which someone is incautious and screws up, or "falls" as it were, into error.

Recalling Michael's discussion of falling as a class distinction is useful, too, when thinking about ableist and sizeist views that decree "normal" adult bodies don't have an argument with gravity. What's the dividing line between maintaining another person's class distinction via "civil inattention" and rendering a falling person socially unseeable? Old people and disabled people, women over fifty and drunk people may have already fallen "beneath notice" – who do we see and who do we gloss over? Civil inattention is often not so civil but rather a form of erasure. Canadian writer Dorothy Ellen Palmer wrote a memoir wittily titled *Falling for Myself* in which she discusses her frequent falling because of a congenital condition involving her feet, and her eventual use of a cane and then a wheelchair. Palmer uses the reality and the metaphor of falling to discuss her own adolescent ableism in which she blamed herself for her unsteadiness, and her hard-earned turn toward body positivity, disability rights and life in a body with important differences. What would it take to fall for yourself? To say that you deserve to be seen both when you are stable and when you are not?

This question is at the core of Amy Sharrocks's 2013 live artworks that involve Sharrock and others staging deliberate falls in order to explore physical experience, emotional currents and social reactions to falling. In her exhibition notes on the Royal British Society of Sculpture's website, Sharrocks noted that falling is an "act of vulnerability, an attempt to understand falling as the natural way of things," and her work "questions the feelings of exposure and shame in being un-surefooted." One of her live art pieces is titled *Invitation to Fall*. In it, Sharrocks went to World's End Place in the Chelsea district of London and invited others to join her in a mass fall. In a 2017 video interview for the European arts organization Create to Connect, Sharrocks made it clear that she is not interested in hurting anyone, and that she invites people to experience consciously, as a matter of choice, an experience to which they have not been conscious. Is an intentional fall still a fall? Others in the "falling group" that Sharrocks put together suggested that a planned fall is more like a drop, that the intention is controlled even when the movement can't be. In her "study guide for falling," Sharrocks proposes five phases to falling: Approach, Letting Go, Falling/Out of Control,

Crash, Recovery. She also exhibited a live art piece titled *Flop*, in which participants staged a mass fall at the corner of Old Brompton Road and Cranley Gardens in London, an urban area deliberately chosen for its foot traffic. Sharrocks's exhibition notes describe *Flop* as "un-shaming the fall on a busy public pavement as a wave of exploring vulnerability and the difficulty of being horizontal while others are vertical." She began this live art falling because it was "the scariest thing I could possibly do," but found that "claiming the right to be ungainly" was a hinge to being vulnerable, and that the truly civil attention of allowing one person from the fall to resist instant recovery, to dwell horizontally for a few seconds or a minute, reminds people of the kind of effort it takes to remain upright.

My entry into ungainliness was adolescence; I grew tall very fast the year I was ten, and for years every adult commented on my height, their discomfort palpable. But hearing Sharrocks discuss "the right to be ungainly" jolted me; it provided me with a positive connotation for that word, so inured had I become to its shaming tone in the discussion of femininity, where gracefulness is considered not only de rigueur but "natural." Alexander Technique, a body work technique to handle stress responses, advocates falling prevention by maintaining a long straight neck, and keeping your head "up and forward" rather than bent, which pulls your head "down and back." The "down and back" position pulls the body backwards when walking so it becomes unstable and is much more likely to result in a painful backwards fall. The "up and forward" head position promotes a forward-facing fall that is much more easily managed, or even corrected without missing a step – a fall that is not a fall. If a "feminine" stance is construed as having downcast eyes and a bashful or retiring demeanour, gracefulness will be hard to maintain; the long straight neck is more likely to result in "gracefulness," but as a position it is more confident and even more confrontational.

It's hard to think about falling as a research event without thinking about the types of bodies that fall. For instance, Mike Michael writes about his age and his understanding of masculinity as a result of his fall, partly inspired by his son's level of distress at seeing his robust father as frail. In my case, I felt my age and femaleness acutely in the ungainly Vancouver wipeout: a peculiar gracelessness of falling with my breasts and hips thrown out of alignment, my memories of falling in a slim girl's body and the shame of skidding out of control while wearing completely ordinary footwear. But then again, maybe strappy sandals, no matter how flat-soled, are like so many fashions designed for women, hobbling by design and hazardous by proxy. A lesbian friend once said to me while eying my footwear, "You straight chicks have it tough." They weren't wrong.

Walking Stumbling Limping Falling by Phil Smith and Alyson Hallett includes Hallett's "score for falling" as a musical event, and an abecedarian poem, "An Alphabet of Falling," composed by both Smith and Hallett. For many abecedarian poems, finding a word for X is the big challenge, but Smith and Hallett note "X marks the spot where you will fall next." I like both of these ways of organizing how we think about that chaotic moment, that shock of a suddenly changed perspective. Could there be a way of falling that allows for a meeting between self and ground that isn't humiliating or judged as unstable? What if our bodies weren't "bad" or "clumsy" or "uncooperative" but better at letting go of stiff uprightness, at being unashamedly less controlled? What if we acknowledged the presence of ungainliness in the world?

Hallett is right – the fear of falling is often worse than the actual fall. I'm not talking about the elderly or those who could be seriously injured by a fall but rather of Michael's "mis-step" as a research event: a way of examining the shakeup of our ordinary perspectives, the step as a bodily event in an ongoing cycle of uprightness and fallenness. And how such a misstep is received is crucial. Jenny Bruso is the founder of Unlikely Hikers, an organization that promotes outdoor adventuring for all kinds of bodies, not just young, fit white people. Bruso writes extensively about outdoor hiking for people who for a variety of reasons (for example, age, sexuality, gender, injury, chronic conditions, body type and neurodiversity) are not what Bruso calls "antelope people." In her body-positive essay "Fat Woman Falling," Bruso notes that hiking became a form of meditation for her when she realized that she could do it her way: "It's presented to us as this thing that will 'fix' what's 'wrong' with our bodies. We aren't told it just feels good. It makes our bodies work better, our minds clearer, our sleep better." Bruso has written eloquently about others' perceptions of her size when engaging in outdoor pursuits, and most poignantly after she fell more than once when snowshoeing in the woods with several other hikers who she didn't know well. This story has a good ending: she fell, she was offered help and received it, and instead of blaming the fall on her size, the more experienced snowshoers took care of her and discovered that she fell not because of her size or her fitness level but because she was wearing the wrong size snowshoes. She fell again after getting the right size of snowshoe, but it wasn't so bad, knowing that the others had her back.

She writes about what it takes to feel the vulnerability of falling in her body: "Being a fat outdoorsperson putting myself out there, really *out there*, for the purpose of disrupting the common narrative."

*

I tripped while running a Terry Fox 10 K. Just after the five-kilometre marker, the boy in front of me stopped running, threw up his arms in victory and yelled, "Finished!" I was not finished; I was in mid-stride with five kilometres still to go. I swerved as soon as my front foot hit the ground, twisted my torso and stumbled around the boy – who was maybe nine years old – without plowing into him, without even touching him.

I kept going. My experiences with awkwardness held true. Chalk one up for the ungainly.

*

One day on a city sidewalk, a young woman veered unsteadily toward me before she fell against a parked car, pulled herself upright and then plunged into traffic and disappeared. I ran to where I'd seen her last and found her unhurt but splayed against the side of a car stopped at the light. I steered her back to the sidewalk; she didn't seem to register that she was in danger. She kept upright as she staggered, though she weaved from side to side whenever I let go of her. I asked if she was all right and got no answer. I drew her to a bench to sit down; she wouldn't, just weaved away. I caught up with her and asked if I could get her water, or coffee, or anything so she would stop. No answer. Wordless, she was determined to stumble her way down the sidewalk. And eventually she did, because unless I wanted to wrestle her to the ground and sit on her, I couldn't stop her. I couldn't even be sure she could hear me. I felt like a thwarted sheepdog standing there, watching her veer away – an unfair comparison, as she was very much a human being making human choices and refusing assistance, as was her right. The fall was hers to take, and I couldn't be her saviour.

I wasn't happy with this outcome, which is why, in part, she still weaves through my mind decades later. Amy Sharrocks notes that as human beings, "our edges are more malleable and more permeable" than we tend to consider in our everyday interactions, and that her work "is about looking at our edges" and the ways in which they may soften – for a few seconds, for a minute, forever. The attention I paid to the veering woman shook me; I wasn't prepared to have my assistance refused, and when it was, I felt permeable, shocked out of my civic urban resilience and into a softness that was deeply uncomfortable. I don't know for certain what her circumstances were. She could have been stoned, or she could have gone off her medication, or she could have been lost in her mind in the aftermath of an assault. When I was the falling person, I appreciated the shout, "Whoa, what a wipeout!" because someone had seen my reality and named it. But when I was trying to help the veering woman, I couldn't name her reality. I could only read her determination; she wanted to keep moving.

*

Vulnerable appears in Smith and Hallett's "Alphabet of Falling" alongside a simple statement: "I can break." I can break, but will I? Hallett writes about feeling proprietary about a route that she had walked many times before, and how, when walking that route after a hip replacement, she took refuge in its familiarity and thought of it as "her" trail. At the end, she fell and was unhurt but strangely exhilarated by the experience and how it proved that pride really did come before a fall. She was glad, too, that her hip replacement functioned well: "My hip was just fine. It was in place, the muscles had reunited in holding it there. . . . I was just a fallen woman and in that moment a fallen woman was a great and liberating thing to be." Falling as a corrective: remember, nothing belongs to you, not even balance.

Hallett's work on how to "foreground ways of walking and be-ing that are not sure-footed" seems radical – it flies in the face of society's insistence on uprightness, and her list of verbs to describe the presence of irregularities in walking reads like a catalogue of my walking life: "To stumble. To stutter. To topple. To tremble. To stagger." The broad association of walking with endurance, distance and athleticism fails to consider that many people walk in more troubled circumstances, or in bodies that may (or may not) strive for smoothness and confidence but have to be satisfied, for at least a period of time, with moving in more tentative ways. Hallett again: "So much of the work connected with walking doesn't seem to explore the wide vocabulary of how a walk can happen." Hallett's *how* is the salient word for me, describing the circumstances under which a walk happens AND the manner of one's body as a self in motion, including the potential for tripping, slipping, stumbling, recovering balance and, of course, falling.

Falling can be political in its performance and intentions. Helene Vosters's *Haunting the Past's Present: Falling for the Forgotten (and not) Dead of History* was performed on the Stanford University campus in June 2013. Using bodies as "spaces that see," in Lia Halloran's terms, Vosters invited public participation in a daylong performance of falling in remembrance of someone who had died, especially someone whose death had been too little acknowledged or honoured, or even refuted or ignored. This is what Vosters calls "an embodied investigation of the space between 'Us' and 'Other,' between personal ritual and public protest." In her invitation to participate, posted on her website, Vosters notes that people could choose to fall once or several times, as their interest or ability allows. For multiple fallers, she requests that they move through dedicating their first fall to a personal loss, then the second fall to a less-personal loss and finally moving to honour the loss of people the faller does not know, members of "a population whose loss, or losses, have been largely disavowed, or minimized, by dominant discourses and processes of memorialization." For this project, the vulnerability of the fallers echoes the vulnerability of the lost, not only the actual loss of life but also the "intention that [the fallers] bring to the risk." The fallers were instructed by Vosters to lie on the ground for thirty minutes before getting up and either (a) leaving or (b) dedicating themselves to another fall.

"Falling unsettles the world," says Amy Sharrocks, and those who have fallen, by accident or by design, feel the jolt. Part of Helene Vosters's work is to have the jolt of forgotten deaths register in at least three ways: with the spoken dedication of the fall to an un/remembered person, with the act of the fall itself and with the maintenance of the fallen body in public for thirty minutes. Falling had better unsettle the world. If it doesn't, we are more lost than we know.

*

The final entry in Smith and Hallett's "Alphabet of Falling" is "Zeno's Paradox" reconfigured for falling: "no one ever completes a fall, for all bodies, when dropping, are always a half of the shrinking distance to the ground, then a half again; we get closer and closer but we never reach our destiny."

Except if you are a barnacle gosling, who before she learns to fly leaps off a shear rocky cliff hundreds of metres above the beach and ocean. The gosling will spread her featherless wing-stubs and descend in a controlled fall – falling as near-flying, until she crashes into the rocks and tumbles the rest of the way down. A YouTube video from BBC Earth shows this process, complete with the parental pair showing up at the bottom of the cliff to meet the gosling. The astonishing part is not that some goslings die this way; that is to be expected. It's that approximately half of the brood will live to adulthood after this brutal start beyond the nest. Maybe Zeno's Paradox is right: the gosling's first drop implies a harsh destiny, but despite hitting the rock, many of the goslings don't die that way. Instead, they learn to fly and fall for the rest of their lives.

Falling in Place

Fall from a kneeling position, collapse sideways onto a cushy carpet:

Relaxing the left side of my legs and torso I descend in pieces first knee to thigh, hip to rolling torso to shoulder to head. My legs curving up as my head hits the carpet, a rocking arc, then flop down. Get up. Fall again. Get up. Fall again. Again. And again. Relax the legs for more flop and less curving roll. Fall better, fail better. *Worstward ho!* Samuel Beckett knew.

Fall through all points of the body, enact the musical score for falling, each point of contact a musical note. Be less careful, be safe.

Get up. Fall again. Get up. Twelve times and it's getting easy. Switch sides.

Right side: can't do it. Can't even begin. I relax the right side of my legs and torso. No, I don't. My body doesn't budge. It's like there's a concrete wall where the air above the carpet moves with its dust motes.

Lie down on my back. Lift head, let it go. Repeat and repeat and repeat. Graduate to shoulder and head flop, then upper-body flop from elbow.

Right. Up on knees again, right side and go.

Nothing.

Fall backwards onto a bed:

First from sitting, an easy dissembling of limbs and spine. A little bounce from the mattress an extra surge of momentum.
Stand up, turn your back to the bed. And tilt your body back, straight as a board. Arms crossed, or arms out like on a cross. Keep the firmness through the hips and torso, don't clench, don't collapse. Think of diving.
Eyes open, eyes closed. Always a second where I just keep falling. Through the bowels of the earth. The stomach flip. Then the bounce of the mattress.

Fall outdoors, months after your first experiment, in an effort to make your fall subtly public in your backyard:

I get ready (gentle, go gentle on the joints). And let go, though I protect my head. I am lying on my side (left, of course) eye level in grass, getting the rabbit's eye view. Not as free with the limbs as I should have been in the fall, a bit of a flop failure, but I don't move. Black-eyed Susans gigantic. Scent of crushed grass where my body's squashed it. Soccer practice, baseball outfields. Running with my friend Cindy when the school bell ran and one of us slipped, then got up scraped and maybe bleeding, and ran on.

Night Walk with Sandra

I walked away from my boyfriend mid-date one night in Winnipeg, and my friend Sandra came with me.

We were sitting outside the Bridge Drive-In in my boyfriend's parents' acid-green Volvo. I was seventeen, and so was Sandra, who was in the back seat. My boyfriend – I'll call him Pete – was eighteen and at the wheel. We had eaten ice cream out on the bridge over the Red River, watching the water rush by below us. I wanted my boyfriend to like my friends, and I wanted to like his friends. But that evening, Pete was sullen. Maybe Sandra and I were having too much fun. Pete didn't like my rambunctiousness; or rather, sometimes he loved it, but other times he'd sourly disapprove of my high spirits, goofing around and girlish laughter. Sometimes his pomposity annoyed me enough that I was happy to push the envelope. It's safe to say that I was too extra for him.

At that age, my experience was that opposites didn't attract but they could envy each other into a relationship. Going out with Pete meant seeing someone whose socio-economic bracket was a discernible step above mine. His parents' privilege gave him a firm foothold on the kind of life I was working hard to attain. My big goal of getting a university degree was going to be as easy as breathing for him.

I didn't really know how to be a girlfriend; I barely knew how to be a girl. I definitely didn't know how to read some of the social cues his parents gave me. But I knew enough to see when I had mis-stepped, and on those occasions I spent too much time calculating the difference between throwing caution to the wind and agoniz-ing over my mistakes. This kept me off-balance. Pete was no more experienced than I was, and in many ways, he had been sheltered by his parents' educational and social status, but he liked it when I overthought things; it gave him a chance to pontificate. He was not a gloater, but he liked to speak didactically, parentally, sagely about what was proper. That's expected in a forty-year-old; in an eighteen-year-old, it wasn't a good look.

I've forgotten what the issue was, mostly because Pete so often wore a disapproving look – when I danced to songs he didn't like, when I wanted to go somewhere he didn't know, when he thought I was too messy or too insistent. If he had been sullen on the bridge, he settled for pursed-lip disapproval in the Volvo – not a rant or shout-ing or scary threats but the steady drip-drip-drip of finger-wagging. Pete was smart and well-read and could be funny, but his stodginess was puzzling. By that night, I had already argued with him about classist statements he'd made about people with university degrees being "better people," about my behaviour and what I wore, about my plans for the future and even about money. If you think that these are arguments you might have with your parents, you are right.

The BDI – say it fast and it'll sound like *beady eye* – boasted ice cream treats like "upside-down shakes" and sundae concoctions like the Goog Special, the Peach Velvet and the mysterious Spanish cone. My dad had a serious sweet tooth, and he loved ice cream; his two all-time favourite places to go were the Dutch Maid ice cream parlour and the BDI. His flavours were maple walnut, butter pecan and rum raisin; he cycled through them with regularity. As Pete droned on about responsibility or respectability, I sat beside him swiftly aging into a woman who rolled her eyes and said, "Yes, dear." I felt like a big cloth bag of dullness was being lowered over my head while we sat parked in front of the place where my dad had taken me to eat ice cream and look at the river. The juxtaposition was grating. And my friend was in the back seat. It's one thing if your boyfriend bores you with inappropriate scolding, wanting you to be more like his idea of a girl – smaller, sweeter, more compliant – but it's another thing if he bores your friend. Suddenly I understood the phrase *bored to tears.*

Sandra and I had been friends for two years. We'd both started at a new school in grade ten and found a group of friends who liked reading and writing and art and theatre. Like me, Sandra had parents who were older than those of our friends, and we talked more than once, morbidly, about the possibility of their early deaths. Sandra could draw and paint, and I could write; we both loved drama class. Sandra was buxom where I was rail-thin; she looked curvy and womanly in a sundress while I looked bony and barely adolescent. She got average grades; I was a brain. My mother always called Sandra "vivacious," and it's true that her good cheer was nearly inexhaustible. I knew more about being a friend than I did about being a girlfriend, but I could be bossy, especially in a group of young women who had big ideas about art and no ideas about how to access it. We were feminists but had nearly no language with which to argue for or defend that position, and though we tried valiantly, we often failed.

And there we were. I looked over at Pete, sporting his infuriating "I know best" face, his lower lip stuck out like a bulldog's while he nodded at his own sagacity. I stared out at the beautiful evening, the canopy of elms swishing high above, people walking with their kids, and me, stuck in a car with this boring young fart and the thought of another summer evening wasted on his pompous sourness. It was just. Too. Much.

I turned to Pete who was in mid-drone. "Cut it out, or I'm walking home."

Pete scoffed, a lip-flapping grunt. I said it again, and added a dangerous phrase: "I mean it." And he laughed. I stared at him. What made him think he had the power to keep me there? I opened the car door, said, "Come on, Sandra, let's walk," and just like that we were walking away from the car together. I was not afraid of Pete, and when he shouted something after us – "Good riddance!" or "Come back!" – I didn't think anything of it. He could get out of the car, walk over and apologize, or he could sit in his attitude and fume. He was an adult; he could choose for himself. Sandra and I walked down Jubilee Avenue; once outside the gravitational pull of the Volvo, we were unhurried. At the lights, we turned right onto a long curving drive that led to a riverside park. It was about 8:00 p.m. in July and the sun was not yet down.

There's something good about walking through a dark night with your friend, even if you don't know which of you might be Dante and which Virgil, even if you are too young to know the difference and even if the inferno that you pass through is familiar. Sandra and I often hung out in a group of friends, and as we walked, we talked as we usually didn't get a chance to. Of course, our first subject was how annoying Pete was, and then, since we easily agreed on that, we turned to other topics: school and friends and the play we were in, the student newspaper, movies and our teachers. Sandra had become a cadet in the last year, but she found it less interesting than she expected and was thinking of quitting, so we talked about that. She was loopy over a guy from another school who seemed to be in love with himself in the manner of cartoon strongmen who kiss their own biceps, so we talked about that. We strolled the length of the park's three-kilometre curve, in no special rush. Pete did not follow us, or if he did, we didn't see him. When we reached the easternmost part of the curve, the sun was lower in the sky and while it was still warm, I noted that we were about eight kilometres away from home. I planned our route back with the authority of someone who had driven that distance countless times, and truth be told, I was eager to tackle them on foot. I had completed a thirty-kilometre walkathon by myself the year before, so I thought those eight kilometres – through the velvety prairie night on streets I knew really well – were not dangerous and would be only the smallest kind of adventure with its sense of stolen time and independence, away for once from the patriarchal rehearsals of teenage boys and travelling under our own power.

As I grew older, I would have much bigger and much worse arguments with lovers, with tears and snot and recriminations in public places. During these arguments, I would step out of cars and take the bus, the subway or a cab home. I would step out of cars and be coaxed back in for decidedly chilly rides home. I wouldn't own a car myself until I was thirty, and when I did, it changed everything. But on this long summer evening, I was elated by the simplicity of walking away. The green of the park rolled away from my feet toward the trees and the river. People were running, walking, playing soccer and Frisbee, and with my friend by my side, the one who came with me without question, I felt light as air.

The grit that Sandra provided by being in the car – and then out of the car – with me was important; I felt that for once I had backup and that my act of exiting the car would have a reliable witness and, if she chose to come with me, a companion. That act of leaving the car may have been a long time coming, but it was accomplished in only a few seconds. I didn't have a real plan after that, but I meant what I said; I was fully capable of walking home. I didn't realize that I wasn't giving Sandra much choice, that she could either come with me or sit in the car with Pete. Hobson's choice, it's called, when there's really only one thing on offer.

*

Sandra got married a few years later, not to the boy who was in love with himself but to a very nice guy. Still, I cried at the wedding – not because it was beautiful or because I was so happy for her but because I saw her freedom slipping away, into a house in the suburbs, and it filled me with a horrible grief. She didn't feel that way at all, giggling as she tossed her bouquet straight at me. I backed away like it was full of snakes, and a crowd of young women leaped into its path and fought for it. Friends don't always want the same thing.

But on the night of the walk, we were two young women out at night in the time before cellphones; we might have been carrying as much as ten dollars between us. We could've caught a bus, but we didn't. It didn't occur to either of us to call a cab, even when we passed a phone booth. Cabs were part of the adult world, and I'm not sure I'd ever taken one at that point in my life – certainly not by myself or with another kid. Neither of us wanted to call our parents; we wanted to solve this ourselves. We walked because we'd grown up walking to and from school. We were pragmatic girls from working-class families, and we agreed that the inconvenience of the walk was well worth the freedom and the statement. We were naive, but this time, anyway, we got away with it; we got away with daring to walk, with daring to make our own choices, with daring to pass through space.

Jubilee Avenue, where the Bridge Drive-In still stands, is named for Queen Victoria's Diamond Jubilee. But as we headed west toward home, the names of places became a little more inflected with Indigenous culture and people. The biggest road we'd cross was Pembina Highway, named for Fort Pembina, the North West Company's trading post in North Dakota. The highway was developed from an ox-cart trail that followed the Red River south toward the fort, which is now a town that advertises itself as the "oldest settlement in the Dakota territories." *Pembina* comes from an Ojibwe word for the highbush cranberry, which Indigenous peoples (and my settler mother) used every year in jams and jellies. Sandra and I would cross Grant Avenue, too, named for the Métis leader Cuthbert James Grant, and just as Pembina Highway remembers a route, Grant Avenue goes all the way out of the city to the west, leading to Grant's community of St. François Xavier.

But because we were white girls who had been raised in colonialism, we didn't know this – or much of it – yet. Our niceness compelled us to take a detour of a few blocks, to walk by Pete's house; if the car was parked out front, we'd stop in and make peace. I might've told him that he shouldn't be so stuffy. And *yes, we're fine, thanks for asking*. But the car was not parked out front, so we kept walking down Pete's residential street and back past the BDI, which was still bustling with customers. We took the pedestrian sidewalk under the cloverleaf of Pembina Highway – the most urban part of our walk – and passed the big Manitoba Hydro building. We passed the schoolyard where I played softball for three years and then by the Pan Am Pool. Sandra and I both learned to swim there; Sandra earned her life-saving certificate when she was fifteen, the youngest you could be and take the course. We wove through a few more blocks to my parents' place and deked down the back lane. The entire walk had taken a little under two hours – with digressions and rests – and it was not even 10:30 p.m.

I leaned into the back porch, hooked my dad's car keys into my hand and drove Sandra home; we were a bit cold, and any drama that the evening held had long since drained away. But we were still talking, and even sat in her driveway for a few minutes to finish our conversation. When I arrived back home for the second time, my mother came to the kitchen and said, "Pete was here." Despite the fact that Pete saw us entering the park and that we had walked a straight route along a path that was visible from the road, he told my mother that he couldn't find us. To hear him tell it, we had vanished into thin air. He sat in my parents' living room, saying, "I've lost her!" When my mother said this, I laughed, incredulous; he lost me like I was a wallet. I also felt sad for the first time that night; sad that I was so unfathomable to my boyfriend, and that we couldn't figure out what seemed so simple: how to treat each other well.

When I think of this now, I am amazed by the flatness of the aftermath. My mother wanted to know what had happened, but she wasn't especially worried. My dad didn't even wake up. My mom liked Pete well enough, but when I said I didn't like how he was treating me, that I had gotten out of his car, she believed that my choice was right. Pete and I did not last long after that. I don't know if Pete was begging for my mother's forgiveness the way he would never beg for mine, or if he was performing distress to save himself and rat me out as a bad girlfriend. But I was infuriated by the new excuse that he'd shrugged himself into: *Chicks, who can tell what they're thinking?*

Yeah, who could guess that "I mean it" means "I mean it"? Women are downright *cryptic*.

*

Partway through writing this, I found Sandra's mother's obituary online: she had lived to a spectacularly advanced age and passed away only a few years ago. My mother, before she died in 2015, would often laugh about the night I was "lost," though she knew I never was. I remembered Sandra telling me on our long walk that she wanted to get married young so she wouldn't be alone when her parents died. She also wanted kids in a way that I did not.

I didn't look online for Pete.

At Sandra's wedding, she hugged me in her lace gown and her veil puffed up against my face in a cloud. I hugged her back as hard as I could, and then she was off on her rounds, embracing each guest in turn. I wondered how soon I could make my exit, but I tricked myself into joining conversations and stayed late enough to see her leave the reception for her honeymoon. She was wearing what used to be called a going-away outfit: hers was a sky blue skirt suit that matched her new husband's tie. I kissed her and wished her luck; she was my friend and I meant it. Sandra and I had threaded our way through the city at night, and I think of our route as though it's marked on a map, with the phosphorous of our bones trailing behind us, glowing just slightly after all these years. What if the molecules in the walking feet and swinging arms of young feminists were bioluminescent, if the energy we released took the form of light? What if every time a young woman walked away from someone who wanted to make her small, the trail glowed and stayed that way, neither perilous nor impossible?

My Dogs Are Barking

For L, ma belle

We walked over the Brooklyn Bridge and passed a man with a Burmese rock python around his neck. We walked from North Beach to Fisherman's Wharf. We walked the 5th and 6th arrondissement in Paris and through Selfoss looking for Bobby Fischer's grave. We walked miles through farmers' markets and outdoor stalls, lugged home cheese and four different kinds of olives. We stood knee-deep in Little Qualicum, walked downhill to the Eygues to bodysurf. We hiked to the dam in St. Jacobs where we heard shots and hoped they were target practice. We were hiking somewhere in the Cariboo when we heard a grizzly roar, up Mauna Kea looking for honeycreepers and finding a wild boar. We were in the Carolinian forest finding turkey tail fungi when you said, "Don't turn your ankle! I promised your mother." I saw snow on your eyelashes in a blizzard by the creek. We have stood beside each other in pharmacies the world over and gazed rapturously at corn pads and moleskin for blisters. Shared foot pain is a love language.

Figure and Ground

An Ecopoetic Travelogue

> If it is the case that our inner lives echo the ebbs and flows of growth and decay in the natural world around us, how can we learn to understand the inner by being closer to the outer?
> – Terry Gifford, "Gary Snyder and the Post-Pastoral"

> It's interesting how you can brag about a scar;
> nothing in nature is a straight line.
> – Gwendolyn MacEwen, "Appendectomy"

JUNE: *growth and decay*

Proposal: to consider the ecopoetic practice tied to moving one woman (poet, performer, professor) from one city to another. There are ecological tire tracks made by driving, shipping and owning a houseful of objects, but as I pack and give away, pack and give away, I wonder about subtler forms of bioregionalism. What kind of toll will such a change take on an aging, breathing, desiring body? How will my body adapt to living in a different space? There will be two of us undergoing this move, so I will have another body against which to measure mine, a comparison necessarily flawed by variables. For

191

instance, my partner (photographer, linguist, philosopher) is by training and nature unflappable; such a description could rarely, if ever, be applied to me. In any case, this trip will have two figures moving over ground, or two figures emerging from ground: two vertical people travelling the horizontal world of the Prairies into the populous maelstrom of Ontario. My partner will also drive a lot of the trip, leaving me to manage details and to overthink the poetics of changing space. The inarguable fact that this will require attention to physical experience is annoying to me – as annoying, I am sure, as I have been to my more cerebral writing students when I advise them to "write through the body," to concretize their imagery, to give their work physical immediacy. I am hoisted by my own petard; as Ken Garnhum writes, "I love irony, unless it's about me." Everything about this move screams physical immediacy, and I am suspicious of the intensity of experience it offers. Having done a cross-country move six years earlier, I am also skeptical of the idea of the road trip as revelatory, or at least, as simplistically so. I am thinking of Daphne Marlatt more than Jack Kerouac. I am thinking of the son in Marlatt's *How Hug a Stone* who cannot breathe in England, his immune system attacked by his ancestral homeland. In *The Poetics of Space*, Gaston Bachelard identifies the kind of absolutism that divides the outer world from the inner world as ontological, and one of the first conversations that must be had by any artist thinking about the relationship between the inner world of the body and the outer world of spatial economies: "To make the inside concrete and the outside vast is the first task, the first problem . . . we shall come to realize that the dialectics of inside and outside multiply with countless diversified nuances."

Is it the dialectic that dogs me, or the nuances? I know that the mere conception of a body moving through space without flying apart is so incredible that I may never get over it. My incredulity is worrisome, though I like to think that I come by it honestly. In

Thinking Through the Body, Jane Gallop warns that relying solely on a poetics of experience comes perilously close to having no poetics at all, particularly "if we understand poetry to be that effect which finds a loophole in the law of the symbolic." The cross-country trip, so lauded in literature and film, seems to me to be a kind of trial by road, and I think that the only way I'll live through it is to cram my body through that loophole and wriggle out into the lawless light. I am prepared to throw away half of what I own or to play *Tetris* in packing it all, but there's no time to choose. Some patterns exist in order to gesture toward deviation. I book our hotel stops along the way and can feel my hands shaking as I put down the phone.

JUNE 29: WINNIPEG TO THUNDER BAY: *closer to the outer*

We buy a full tank of gasoline early in the morning to drive over the Ontario border and enter the Shield. I gaze into the middle distance as I pump the gas; I squint and act the untouchable traveller handling a renewable resource, but I am queasy with eco-shock as I replace the gas cap. Before we reach the provincial border, I count three deer brave enough, or starved enough, to forage close to the road. Two lay dead. One raises her head and bounds away from the car. I know that we're driving toward a boundary that is not only geographical and rhetorical but also something larger and yet more intimate, something that will alter my material practice. Why does this particular way of moving through space seem to augur something terrible? The press of brush on either side of the highway reminds me that we are travelling too fast to note individuality and yet the individuality of every living thing seems to reach for me. I am caught in a phenomenological fever dream, and having the language to describe it only makes me dizzier.

On the move, time is deceptive and deeply relative. The natural world is steady: a glacier, a rock, a trained runner. The natural world is also sudden, and does not ask for human permission: the sound of thunder, organ rejection, hail. In order for change to occur – and change must occur in all living organisms – an object must pass through one space on its way to another, either altered by attention (ecstatic, erratic, ecopoetic) or remaining immune to such influence. It is the poet's job to discern and point out the links between ways of seeing, speaking and writing – bridges between one world and another, between two frightened and angry people, between the woman jogging on the back road and the badger on whom she nearly steps. I think of the swamps and sloughs I waded through in all my years of childhood camping, then the bloom of algae and the un-swimmable beaches, the crowds and the electrical hookups, *Hockey Night in Canada* blasting leaves off poplars. What is happening to the space I move through? I am thinking about the country – I mean the nation-state known as Canada, of course, but I also mean the stretches of land we used to call "the country," as in "My cousin's farm is out in the country near Deloraine." One generation removed from that farmland, my brother and I used to howl with laughter at the dwindling population of my mother's birthplace of Wakopa, Manitoba. "Population: 27," its peeling sign said sometime in the 1970s. The sight of the falling-down buildings against the parched land all around us, coupled with the thought that this was somewhere our mother had lived, struck us, two city kids, as the height of hilarity. It's not funny now, as we drive through the country and I look at each town's toehold on the economy.

*

Define: *ecopoetics*. Define: *praxis*. Poetic scholarship, or scholarly poetics? From seed catalogues and the laugh of the Medusa, I thought I knew how to grow a female poet, but I have transplanted myself so often that I'm starting to worry about what echo this poetics sounds throughout my body: tripping, bruised, exhausted?

Entropy is the law of the body. There are a million ways to be in a body, and a million ways to write it. All my books on feminist theory are in boxes in the trunk of my Buick, and now there's only my body riding beneath my ventriloquist brain, which cites and figures endlessly. Writing from the body is good advice; I just don't always know how to apply it to my body. Like a bandage, like lotion, like copper for arthritis? My reflexivity has a sprained ankle; it limps. My body enters mourning the moment the provincial boundary is crossed, and will not listen to logic, maps or necessity. Leonard Cohen wrote, "If your life is burning well, poetry is just the ash." Do I want a well-burning life? Like petroleum. Like a cigarette, a crematorium. Oil fields.

I've lived all over Canada, and studied its literature and history, and still, on this trip, the land punches me like a clock. Wordsworth wrote that "Nature never did betray / The heart that loved her," but we should never forget that Nature's love is not for the faint of heart. Donna Haraway reminds us that when we speak about our love for nature, we must remember that "love is relentlessly particular, specific, contingent, historically various, and resistant to anyone having the last word." Oh, that last word, how I want it, despite all appeals to love or deconstruction. Nature's not for burning. I'm not allergic, not even to change, but there's something hostile here, and I think it's me. When I wasn't looking (or maybe when I was), I became the trapper in Earle Birney's "Bushed." I bar myself in and feel the great flint that is my doubt thwack hard against my heart.

I'll reconfigure my question: Does geography alter praxis? How global is my local(e)? Will this land make me over? Local turning loco. On the mad slingshot of the Trans-Canada Highway, I think about the prospect of growing outside my own garden. Rain sluices the windshield and boxes bump in the car's trunk. We're passing by signs for the small northern Ontario towns where my parents lived when they were young and childless: Dryden, Atikokan, Rainy

River. When it's not my turn to drive, I stare out the window and know that this is no road movie. Am I still writing the body? Haven't I already written it into existence, into concreteness, into a perfectly observable, measurable, livable reality?

JULY 1: CANADA DAY: *it's interesting how you can brag*
We stop at the Terry Fox Monument outside Thunder Bay and watch people from several countries weep at the foot of the statue. Terry ran halfway across the country on one leg in 1980, the year I turned eighteen. Like a friend of mine that year, he had osteogenic sarcoma. Like her, he died from a cancer that is now treatable. The statue reminds me of how a body in peril can pit itself against the land, how it can move through the landscape, figure and ground. Seeing the statue against the dark lake and the felled body of the Sleeping Giant gives me a piece of the puzzle: Writing the body, like writing nature, means writing death. No way to avoid it. Oh, the smug irony, the gap-toothed pride of writing the body. Now that it has ceased to be my manifesto, I envy those who can escape from writing the body. Is envy toxic? It's green. Decay looks like chlorophyll. A static body can fool you by imitating motion. Every body in the world becomes worn down by wind and weather, by time and grief, by hard use and even by joy.

For miles along the road, I see yellow triangular signs with drawings of moose and the words *Night Danger*. Maybe it is the length of the moose's legs, attenuated stilts holding up a massive body and antlered head that make me misread these words over and over as *Night Dancer*. A black bear runs across the road two hundred metres ahead, hurried, aware of the cars and the need to make for the bush. When the moose, the northern Night Dancer herself, launches herself up out of the ditch, it's the legs I notice pushing against the slope – legs used to traversing rough ground and hard climbs, now pushing against the gravity of the ditch by the highway. Figure emerging from ground. Figure crashing into the jeep two cars ahead. Motion meets motion then stasis.

Or worse, a motion that precedes stasis. The moose is on her side on the road's gravel shoulder, kicking her broken back leg, spasmodic, insistent. It's not yet noon. The jeep who hit her is still intact, the people in it climb out, and a tour bus on the other side of the road stops and people pour from it. There is no town for a hundred kilometres in either direction, and looking at the moose, who will never stand again, I know that none of us passing through this space is carrying a gun. My grandfather was an old Canadian National Railway man and a veteran of two wars, and I can hear him make a Scottish noise that sounds like he's about to spit. He'd ask us what good we were, an animal in pain and none of us able to relieve it. The moose's eyes are wild and white as we drive carefully by. There are many miles to go, but the symbol has burst in on me. The moose's eyes say everything about the country and space, about the air and its breathability, about my search for a loophole in the law of the symbolic, about how our experience of the outer changes our understanding of the inner. How else to write an abundance of bodies in various states of productivity or decay? Where there's a body, there are politics; there's no poetry without politics, no pure engagement with language that isn't haunted by bodies heard or unheard.

AUGUST: KITCHENER, ONTARIO: *about a scar*

I am still paying for the moose in attention. I try to turn my struck-silent witnessing of the unmanageable into narrative or poetry, knowing that all my anxieties are frittered away. In southwestern Ontario, natural disaster = tornadoes, and unnatural disaster = Highway 401. I think of the Greenbelt, the swath of land the Ontario government has pledged (as long as rivers run) to keep as farms, parkland or undeveloped wilderness. I drive to this maintained wildness on the screaming highway to hike its gorges, to climb its ridges, to dangle off its escarpment, to get the spectacular view of the city huffing its blanket of smog. I know what's being asked of me because I am the one asking it. Poet Tim Lilburn writes that when he moved back to Saskatchewan, he knew he would have to "learn to bed down where events had brought [him]." It's the lot of the peripatetic to refit the self between strange molecules, to learn how to read new ground, to re-figure oneself in space. In this space, I find a skunk stamping on my lawn at midnight, and listen to the boys in the group home next door arguing about how often to water their one potted geranium on the porch.

There is a science linking logic to poetic practice, and when I think about it, my hair lies quietly on my head, my toenails grow a little faster, my blood swishes cleanly through my veins. Haraway claims, famously, that she couldn't choose between the disciplines of biology, literature and philosophy because to her, all three disciplines seemed to describe the same set of ideas. She regards semiotics as "barnacles that crust" even the most technical of terms, words that in turn become "thick, living, physical objects that do unexpected things." Any sailor knows you can cut yourself on barnacles. That's one of the problems with (and pleasures of) writing poetry in the green and greying world: writing the living, kicking, dying bodies of many; writing with thick, living, physical objects.

SEPTEMBER: *nothing in nature is a straight line*
Every writer needs a cautionary tale about the cost of being too damned clever. In *Left Fields*, Jeanette Lynes writes about her discovery that the forest lining the Trans-Canada Highway is just a thin wall of brush left behind by loggers to trick Canadians into thinking the TCH is a passageway through wild woods. I followed the local creek, Laurel Creek (oh, changed body of Daphne, Arethusa), by bicycle, riding through the subdivisions to find low water in the

millrace, the ducks bobbing there dirty as rats. Nietzsche warned that too often, our use of metaphor can be violent; it fools us into thinking we know something about the object we are describing. What we think we know can be dangerous, tricked out in intellect. The price of a thinking body is eternal vigilance against satisfaction. The price is standing on this ground, without a net. As Lilburn writes, we can learn about where we stand by learning to "read the shit, read the deer trails." Reading the shit: evidence of presence on earth, animal, human. I like that shit, that most Anglo-Saxon word, is a method.

At odds with the odds, home and deranged, writing here and risking everything to be here on land that the government took from the Six Nations and sold to German and Mennonite and Dutch farmers and millers and wheelwrights who gave their names to the grid of streets in this new home city. Here, we have used landfill to make a ski hill; here, we are turning old mattress factories into lofts. My body, my figure on ground is not yet poisoned, nor is it pathogenic. Do I dare eat an Ontario peach grown during a season with a record number of smog days? I could write thirteen ways of looking at the pair of cardinals nesting behind my house, but at least three of those ways include looking at the homeless guy who's living on the bench in the park just beyond the cardinals' elm. The neighbours warn me not to look; they say, "This place is becoming just like Toronto." When I ask about the last time they were in Toronto, they say they never go there. The homeless man looks like he could use a good night's sleep. Here, we are doing the unexpected: we are moving through space, we are growing older, we are sanding the table smooth, we are acting our prairie selves far from home. We are bragging about our scars.

Life List

Life list: a birder's term for a list of species seen in a lifetime.

*

Count the animals you see. Count the
ones you don't. Count the people you
miss. Count heads. A list has mass.
Everything leaves a trace.
A fox shimmers and evaporates.
That which we list persists.
Record and hoard.

*

Spotting scope. Crosshairs.
What's moving in the brush?
Who's game to tally?
When is a list not a list? I won't
work the feathers. Repetition is
the last recluse in the desert.
The purple finches were here, then they were not.
The beautiful boys were here, then they were not.
We can go from tinder to fire in five seconds.

STRAGGLE

*

Life list: a struggle for control of chance: to name, to count, to tab-
ulate.

*

On Kijiji. Wanted: farm for hunting wild
turkey, deer, mourning doves.

*

Moving between one tree and another,
I lost the list. I built the fire.
Now I'm off the rails, so count me in.
I don't know that I fit the description.

*

Horror-film gabble of the loon.
Trees have their own ransom notes to write.
Sunset bloody sunset. Song of myselfmyselfmyself.
I went into the woods because I wanted.
I want into the weep because I wooded.
The fire in my head.
The glowing outline of a deer.

*

Life list: to find a narrative, to remember, to embed.

*

If you find yourself lost in the woods, stay in one place.
Build a fire, for heat and for signalling.
Don't play with the matches.
Sing something.

*

Miss and remiss. The animals are not
a carnival. They are neither
tenor nor vehicle; I cannot
sing their part, I cannot ride this
deer into town. They will not
carry a tune or us. They are not like
anything.

*

What is the difference between a life list and a necrology?

*

The animal article.
A deer. The loon.
The misread sign.
A wrong turn.
Microbes and a virus.
A killdeer. The killed deer.
An A-frame. A T cell.
A boy. And another.
More and more cormorants.
Heron flyby.

*

A list is boring.
A list is baring.
A list is burning.

Works Referenced

Ansuini, Aaron (@AaronLinguini). "*demon tries to inhabit my body*." Twitter, June 5, 2018, 2:43 p.m. https://twitter.com/aaronlinguini/status/1004116559571312640.

Bachelard, Gaston. *The Poetics of Space*. Translated by Maria Jolas. Boston: Beacon Press, 1969.

Benjamin, Walter. "Unpacking My Library: A Talk About Book Collecting." In *Illuminations: Essays and Reflections*, edited by Hannah Arendt, 59–68. Translated by Harry Zohn. New York: Schocken Books, 1968.

Berger, John. *Ways of Seeing*. London: Penguin, 1972.

Bergson, Henri. *Laughter: An Essay on the Meaning of the Comic*. Translated Cloudesley Brereton and Fred Rothwell. New York: Macmillan, 1911.

Brooks, Mel, dir. *Young Frankenstein*. 1974; Los Angeles: 20th Century Fox Home Entertainment, 2006. DVD.

Bruso, Jenny. "Fat Woman Falling." jennybruso.com, May 1, 2017. https://jennybruso.com/2017/05/01/part-i-fat-woman-falling/.

Calder, Alison. "We Hate the Animals." In *Wolf Tree*, 54. Regina: Coteau Books, 2007.

Calvino, Italo. *Invisible Cities*. San Diego: Harvest, 1972.

Cixous, Hélène. "The Laugh of the Medusa." Translated by Keith

Cohen and Paula Cohen. *Signs* 1, no. 4 (Summer 1976): 875–93.

Clevidence, Cody-Rose. "On Writing, Editing and Living in the Wilderness." Interview by Elaine Kahn. *The Creative Independent*, August 15, 2019. https://thecreativeindependent .com/people/poet-cody-rose-clevidence-on-writing-editing -and-living-in-the-wilderness/.

Coleman, Daniel. *Yardwork: A Biography of an Urban Place.* Hamilton: Wolsak and Wynn, 2017.

Derrida, Jacques. "The Animal That Therefore I Am (More to Follow)." Translated by David Wills. *Critical Inquiry* 28, no. 2 (Winter 2002): 369–418.

Frears, Stephen, dir. *The Queen.* 2006; Toronto: Alliance Atlantis, 2007. DVD.

Gallop, Jane. *Thinking Through the Body.* New York: Columbia University Press, 1988.

Garnhum, Ken. *Pants on Fire.* Directed by Duncan McIntosh. Tarragon Theatre, Toronto, March 17–April 17, 1994.

Gifford, Terry. "Gary Snyder and the Post-Pastoral." In *Ecopoetry: A Critical Introduction*, edited by J. Scott Bryson, 77–87. Salt Lake City: University of Utah Press, 2002.

Hallett, Alyson, and Phil Smith. *Walking Stumbling Limping Falling: A Conversation.* Axminster, UK: Triarchy Press, 2017.

Halloran, Lia. *Your Body is a Space that Sees.* 2016–17. Series of large-scale cyanotype works. https://liahalloran.com/your-body -is-a-space-that-sees.

Haraway, Donna J. "Morphing in the Order: Flexible Strategies, Feminist Science Studies, and Primate Revisions." In *The Haraway Reader*, 199–222. New York: Routledge, 2004.

Hynes, Maureen. *Sotto Voce.* London, ON: Brick Books, 2019.

Jacobson, Esther. The Deer Goddess of Ancient Siberia: A Study in the Ecology of Belief. New York: E.J. Brill, 1993.

Kern, Leslie. *Feminist City: A Field Guide.* Toronto: Between the

Lines, 2019.

Kirby. *Poetry is Queer.* Windsor, ON: Palimpsest Press, 2021.

Kroetsch, Robert. *Seed Catalogue.* Winnipeg: Turnstone, 1986.

Lanham, J. Drew. *The Home Place: Memoirs of a Colored Man's Love Affair with Nature.* Minneapolis: Milkweed Editions, 2017.

LaPensée, Elizabeth, and Weshoyot Alvitre. *Deer Woman: An Anthology.* Albuquerque: Native Realities, 2016.

Lee, Janice Jo. *Will You Be My Friend?* Directed by Matt White. Green Light Arts, Kitchener, ON, May 9–20, 2018.

Levertov, Denise. "Come into Animal Presence." In *Poems of Denise Levertov, 1960–1967.* New York: New Directions, 1983.

Lilburn, Tim. "Going Home." In *Thinking and Singing: Poetry and the Practice of Philosophy,* edited by Tim Lilburn, 173–85. Toronto: Cormorant, 2002.

Livingston, John A. *Rogue Primate: An Exploration of Human Domestication.* Toronto: Key Porter, 1994.

Lynes, Jeanette. *Left Fields.* Toronto: Wolsak and Wynn, 2003.

MacEwen, Gwendolyn. *The Poetry of Gwendolyn MacEwen.* Vol. 1, *The Early Years.* Edited by Margaret Atwood and Barry Callaghan. Toronto: Exile Editions, 1993.

Mackey, Eva. *Unsettled Expectations: Uncertainty, Land and Settler Decolonization.* Winnipeg: Fernwood Publishing, 2016.

Macpherson, Jay. "The Third Eye." In *The Boatman,* 7. Toronto: Oxford University Press, 1957.

Maracle, Lee. *My Conversations with Canadians.* Toronto: Book*hug, 2017.

Marlatt, Daphne. *Ghost Works.* Edmonton: NeWest Press, 1993.

Medoro, Dana, and Alison Calder. "Ethics, Activism, and the Rise of Interdisciplinary Animal Studies: An Interview with Cary Wolfe." *Topia: A Canadian Journal of Cultural Studies* 10 (2003): 39–52.

Michael, Mike. "Walking, Falling, Telling: The Anecdote and the

Mis-Step as a 'Research Event.'" In *Walking Through Social Research*, edited by Charlotte Bates and Alex Rhys-Taylor, 128–42. London: Rutledge, 2017.

O'Farrell, Maggie. *I Am, I Am, I Am: Seventeen Brushes with Death.* New York: Knopf, 2018.

Ondaatje, Michael. *In the Skin of a Lion.* Toronto: McClelland & Stewart, 1987.

Palmer, Dorothy Ellen. *Falling for Myself: A Memoir.* Hamilton: Wolsak and Wynn.

Prohom Olson, Danielle. "Doe, a Deer, a Female Reindeer: The Spirit of Winter Solstice." *Gather Victoria*, December 15, 2017. https://gathervictoria.com/2017/12/15/doe-a-deer-a-female-deer-the-spirit-of-mother-christmas/.

Richards, David Adams. *Facing the Hunter: Reflections on a Misunderstood Way of Life.* Toronto: Doubleday Canada, 2012.

Ricou, Laurence. *Vertical Man/Horizontal World: Man and Landscape in Canadian Prairie Fiction.* Vancouver: University of British Columbia Press, 1973.

Ruefle, Mary. *Madness, Rack, and Honey: Collected Lectures.* Seattle: Wave Books, 2012.

Sharrocks, Amy. "An Anatomy of Falling." *Performance Research* 18, no. 4 (2013): 48–55.

———. *Study Guide on Falling.* PDF. November 28, 2012.

Smith, Phil. "Walking in a Time of Virus." University of Plymouth (blog). April 15, 2020. https://www.plymouth.ac.uk/news/pr-opinion/walking-in-a-time-of-virus.

Solnit, Rebecca. *Wanderlust: A History of Walking.* New York: Penguin, 2001.

Surani, Moez. "Current Projects: Some Contemporary Sites of Islamophobia." moezsurani.com. https://moezsurani.com/Some-Contemporary-Sites-of-Islamophobia

Tagore, Rabindranath. *Stray Birds.* New York: Macmillan, 1916.

Thomas, Elizabeth Marshall. *The Hidden Life of Deer: Lessons from the Natural World*. New York: Harper Perennial, 2010.

Thoreau, Henry David. *Walden: Or, Life in the Woods*. Princeton: Princeton University Press, 1971. First published 1854.

Wilson, Elizabeth. *The Sphinx in the City: Urban Life, the Control of Disorder, and Women*. Berkeley: University of California Press, 1992.

Wittgenstein, Ludwig. *Philosophical Investigations*. Translated by G.E.M. Anscombe. Oxford: Blackwell, 2001. First published 1953.

Woolf, Virginia. *The Waves*. London: Hogarth Press, 1931.

York, Alissa. *Effigy*. Toronto: Random House, 2007.

———. *Fauna*. Toronto: Vintage Canada, 2011.

Notes

Epigraph from *Wild: An Elemental Journey* by Jay Griffiths, used with permission from David Higham Associates.

Excerpt from "We Hate the Animals," from *Wolf Tree* by Alison Calder, used with permission.

"This Limp Goes to Eleven" pays homage to "Thirteen Ways of Looking at a Blackbird" by Wallace Stevens.

"Take Daily" took inspiration from "Your Personal Prescription Information" by Sue William Silverman.

"Take Back the Night" riffs on "Take Back Your Mink" by Frank Loesser.

"Life List" remembers John Pfau, Wilf Gaidosch, Peter Leslie, David Horn and Ted Karavidas. I remember being young with you.

Some of these pieces were previously welcomed by the following journals and anthologies. My gratitude to the hard-working editors whom I rarely see in person but whose emails keep me moving between books. It's a pleasure to be read by you.

Contemporary Verse 2 – "Figure and Ground"
Studies in Canadian Literature – "The Trouble with FaunaWatch"
Atlantis – an early version of "Take Daily" as "Prescription"

Prairie Fire – "Take Back the Night"
Release Any Words Stuck Inside of You II – "Crawford Lake" and "There's a raptor rescue . . ."
The New Quarterly – "Walk This Way" and an early version of "This Limp Goes to Eleven" as "Thirteen Ways of Looking at a Limp"
Understorey – "Crazed"
The Fiddlehead – "Ricochet: An Arcade"
The Goose – "Birding for Beginners: an incomplete quiz" and "Syrinx"
Dusie – "At the Medieval Faire . . ." as "Hawks and Handlers"
Sweet Water: Poems for the Watersheds – "A Feminist Guide to Reservoirs"

Acknowledgements

Is it just me or do you always read the acknowledgements? (See: self-selection bias.) Reading a list of who the writer thanks is a strange pleasure, perhaps, but I look forward to seeing how many people thinking together made a book, and who was cooking the meals.

For me, being a poet-essayist feels like a transformation that has been true all along, folk tale crossed with cautionary tale. My first book of essays, *Out of Line*, was born from classroom and community conversations, and I was reasonably sure that the book would find readers based on those beginnings. *Straggle* was an idea simple in conception but complicated in practice: to move through space as the ever-shifting all of me, and to capture those experiences in all their glory and muddy footprints. I talked to a lot of people about how poetry feeds nonfiction writing and vice versa. Yvonne Blomer, in a talk at the Canadian Creative Writers and Writing Programs conference in Fredericton in 2017, called poetry and nonfiction "the best of cousins," which I thought of with hope as I waded into these cousin-infested waters.

No one writes a book by themselves. Books are written in a community of ideas, arguments, other books, other minds, persistent questions and, most importantly, people with whom the writer is lucky enough to listen and talk. Some of this book was written during various versions of lockdown and restricted social conditions due to the COVID-19 pandemic, and I thought a lot – as I bet you did, too – about what it meant to be alone and to be together, and my thoughts on those things shifted weekly. The process threw into sharp relief the generosity and time taken by the people who stood with me as I wrote. Such friendship and collegiality deserves more than a few pages at the end of a book, but I'll begin there and throw a party later.

I wrote most of this book on the traditional territories of the Neutral, Anishinaabe and Haudenosaunee peoples, and I learned to walk in Treaty One Territory, the traditional territory of the Anishinaabe, Cree, Oji-Cree, Dakota and Dene peoples, and the heartland of the Métis people. I grew up drinking water that was sourced from Shoal Lake 40 First Nation. Many thanks to Melissa Ireland and Corri Daniels for their friendship and assistance in learning well during their years working at the Indigenous Student Centre on the Waterloo campus of Wilfrid Laurier University.

The always-generous Eufemia Fantetti gave me the gentle shove to write "Take Daily" at exactly the right time and in exactly the right way: an act of mind-melding that was nothing less than Spock-worthy. Big love to Ariel Gordon, for weekly meetings, first-draft reads and for alerting me to Helene Vosters's work. My brilliant friend Ed Lepieszo showed me the Tagore quotation years ago. Concetta Principe directed me to the information on "deer strikes." Maureen Hynes has been a friend forever and it was a pleasure to spend time with her work. My heartfelt thanks go to Louise Bernice Halfe – Skydancer for her open spirit and her recommendation of Melissa Febos. (And to Melissa Febos, who will never know how important her writing was to me at the right time.)

I am incredibly lucky to meet regularly with a group of writers who provided insightful views and warm support on many of these essays as they developed. Erika Batdorf always said that she wanted more of me, and she gave me a crash course in Alexander Technique so I wouldn't injure myself falling. Ken Wilson shared his essays about walking in Regina along with many, many book recommendations – Ken, I'm still reading these! Thanks to Lisa Richter for her questions, to Kim Fahner for her love and swearing, and to Adrienne Gruber for bringing the genre-crossing energy – poet-essayists unite! Roberta Laurie kept these essays honest and let me premiere "Birdwatching for Beginners" as a guest in her class.

My poetry peeps were happy to discuss the space between prose and poetry: bless you, Laurie D. Graham, Madhur Anand, Pamela Mordecai and Sarah Tolmie for online and in-person meetings, and for helping me bring Daphne to life. Many Electronic Garretians jumped in to push a few of these pieces along during a dark November. My workshop participants at the Sage Hill Writing Experience from 2018 to 2020 inspired me to no end, and I felt lucky to be so creatively shaken up each summer by so many smart and passionate peers. Students in my writing courses at Wilfrid Laurier University kept me on my toes; the more I watch them write, the more I remember to be a writer. I have long been resistant to the popular view that teaching is a fallback position for writers, and while it is undeniable that a regular paycheque is a very good thing, I also know that teaching writers is an honour and reminds me daily that my own writing practice is a privilege that I am not allowed to waste.

In Waterloo, Kat Spring taught me the value of the cemetery walk, and Nathalie Foy reminded me of how often I had boots on the ground in Toronto, my bête noire city and beloved former place. I've walked in so many cities and down so many wooded trails with my bestie, Leena Niemela, that I've lost count, and we have weathered the nearly impossible task of buying shoes together in three states and two provinces.

My trio of feminist health care workers went the distance with me on this book, and my gratitude goes to Shelley, Lisa and Dr. R. for their help in these fragile times.

The wonderful team at Wolsak and Wynn always makes me feel seen. Noelle Allen has the instincts of an osprey, able to spot a book idea from a great height and yank it wriggling from the pond of "what if." Jennifer Rawlinson designed a cover worthy of any and all spark birds. Andrew Wilmot and Ashley Hisson reminded me, once again, that rigorous copy-editing is how writers care for each other.

The editors who published early versions of these essays deserve credit for turning my head to the personal essay and all its forms. Susan Scott took a chance on "Walk This Way," and Katherine Barrett gave "Take Daily" its first airing. Cynthia Sugars published one of the first essays from this book and may not have known what she started. Di Brandt encouraged me to write "Figure and Ground" when it was just a handful of notes.

Extra special thanks to John for the garden, courage, Emma, being the love of my life, teaching me to play chess, saying "Did you walk today?" and everything else. You are so not like the others.

Finally, thanks to everyone who appears in these pages. I see you, and I remember those walks we took and those fights we had and how we made each other laugh.

*

In one of my favourite *Blackadder* sketches, in series two, set in the 1590s, Lord Percy claims that his money problems will soon be over because he has discovered the secret of alchemy, and he is going to be very rich. He reveals a melted lump of metal clutched in his hand and breathes reverently, "Behold. A brooch of purest green."

Writing a book is alchemical and the secret is to love your brooch of purest green.